ONE OF A KIND

DOREEN SALMON

Published by

MELROSE BOOKS

An Imprint of Melrose Press Limited
St Thomas Place, Ely
Cambridgeshire
CB7 4GG, UK
www.melrosebooks.co.uk

FIRST EDITION

Copyright © Doreen Salmon 2009

The Author asserts her moral right to
be identified as the author of this work

Cover designed by Richard Chambers

ISBN 978 1 906561 67 3

Printed and bound in Great Britain by:
CPI Group (UK) Ltd, Croydon, CR0 4YY

FSC
www.fsc.org
MIX
Paper from
responsible sources
FSC® C013604

Acknowledgements

My grateful thanks to the following:

The surgeon and staff at Derriford Hospital, Plymouth, who saved my son's life.

John, the detective in charge of the criminal case that was to follow.

Bury General Hospital, where my son first showed signs of recovery due to the positive and caring attitude that they administered towards him.

The staff at Rakehead Rehabilitation Unit at Burnley General Hospital, with a special thank you to Doctor A, the consultant who took Gary on when no one else would.

Social Services at Chaddesley House, Burnley, who helped to ensure the best possible quality of life for my son.

Special Acknowledgements

To my husband Edwin, my guardian and protector, ever present to wipe away the tears and fold me in his arms.

To my daughter Shelagh, who suffered alongside me, showing a strength of character very few people are capable of. I am so proud of you.

To my brother Keith, who has been there all along and cared for me as only a brother can.

A special mention for my grandchildren, Aaron, Damien, Daniel and Nathan, who have turned out to be fine upstanding young men; a credit to their mother and to society in general.

Last, but not least of all: throughout my journey in life it was my encounter with Jesus that sustained me. My belief in a Living God who was able to help me never faltered. I stood upon a rock that never moved and I drank from a well that never ran dry.

Dedication

This book is dedicated to my son,

Gary Cook.

Unable to talk, I will never know the full extent of your suffering and I will never cease to be amazed at the strength you have shown throughout.

Your smile lights up our lives!

Chapter One

My earliest memory was as a five-year-old. I was sitting on the stairs that divided the living room from the front room. I knew my mother was in the front room, but I was not allowed in. People had been coming and going all day, but my father had told me I was not to go in.

I clearly recall devising a plan. If I sat on the stairs for long enough, people would get used to seeing me there. I would somehow become invisible. And that is exactly what happened. I suddenly found there was no one there, so I made a dash for it – straight through the door of the front room I went, feeling a sense of achievement.

Having gained access, I stood looking at a long box. Lying inside the box was my mother. I immediately tried to wake her up, but to no avail. Screaming and shouting, I tried to get into the box. Then a pair of hands much bigger than mine grabbed me round the waist and hoisted me out. Had I known at the time the cruelty I was to suffer at the hands of my father's next bride, I would indeed have been far better off had I succeeded.

It was at this time my life was to change from being in a normal, loving family to one filled with pain, fear, hunger and neglect.

My brother Keith, who is two years older than me, told me that after my mother died the family held a meeting at my Grandma and Granddad Waddington's house to discuss what to do with us children. We had three uncles and two aunties, plus Grandma and Granddad, so our future should have been pretty secure. After all, we knew them well, they were family and we knew ourselves to be loved by them.

1

The outcome of the meeting was that no one wanted us and we were to be fostered out.

In due course, we went to a Mr and Mrs Bell, who lived in Nelson, Lancashire; not far from the family home. Mr Bell was a major in the army so we didn't see much of him. Mrs Bell was ever present and constantly cruel. This was to be our first taste of what lay ahead. When my aunties visited each Friday on pay day, I clung to them, crying and screaming for them not to leave me there, while Mrs Bell, a sweet smile on her face, told me not to be a silly girl. As soon as my aunties left, the mask slipped; I received a good hiding and was sent to bed with no supper. She was, however, the lesser of two evils. The 'best' was yet to come.

My father worked in the cotton mills, as did all my family. He had a fancy for a fellow worker called Gwendolyn (apparently while my mother was still alive); although I understand she was the one who did all the chasing. I don't know whether my father married her because of us children or simply because he wanted to, but marry her he did, with my mother not long in her grave.

When we returned to the family home, I don't think that I was too concerned about who was there because I was so happy to be back. The first time my brother and I met Gwen, we had been out collecting money for Guy Fawkes' Night by singing, and as a reward we spent two pennies on a pencil and rubber. When we went back home we were very happy because we'd earned quite a bit of money. We stopped in our tracks as our father introduced this stranger as his new wife.

My stepmother was small in stature, with thin legs, enormous bosoms and going bald on top. I don't know what my father saw in her, but, perhaps on reflection, I do.

The first words she spoke to me were, 'Call me Gwen.' I had a real struggle with this because I had been told that I was going to get a new mother. Also, in those days children didn't address grown-ups by their first names, so I was unable to do as she said and the name 'Gwen' was never uttered by me. I shall, however, for the purpose of these writings, call her Gwen. That night, she confiscated our pennies and sent us off to bed.

Doreen Salmon

I soon settled into a routine similar to that of before my mother died, although there were certain things added and others taken away. I had to go to bed earlier and I wasn't allowed the light on (I got round this by leaning over the bed and reading my comics by torchlight). I was not allowed to get myself a biscuit or a drink without asking; if I did it was called stealing and I was punished. I quickly learnt not to steal by way of a strap, which was to become my constant companion.

Chapter Two

I WAS BORN ON 15 JULY 1935 in the then industrial town of Nelson, Lancashire. The main employers throughout the North West at that time were the cotton manufacturers. All my family were employed as weavers, as were most of the local inhabitants, and worked in the mill at the bottom of our street. A 'knocker-up' came round at about five o'clock each morning with a long pole and rattled the bedroom window to make sure the workers were down at the mill in time. They got fifteen minutes for breakfast, half an hour for dinner, and finished at half past five. They couldn't hear anyone talk in the mill; everyone had to learn to lip read because the looms were so noisy. The children started work at the age of fourteen. Most families were poor and glad of the extra money; besides which, education comprised simply of the three Rs: reading, riting (writing) and rithmetic (arithmetic). The powers that be did not consider the working classes worthy of education. As a result of this, few went on to further education and many were available as cheap labour to work in the mills.

Our house was a two-bedroom terrace and it stood in the middle of seven others. The living-room floor consisted of concrete flags covered in lino, which was always cracking because the flags weren't level. We had a small rockery garden at the front and a yard at the back. In the yard was a stone building where we stored our coal, and another building that consisted of a long-drop toilet. We didn't have an indoor toilet. We had no electricity; we had gas lights with mantles that used to burn out and had to be replaced. The house was okay, but we were always cold. It became my job to set the fire. I had to empty the ashes tray and lay paper, wood and firelighters, with coal on the top. When I lit the fire I had to put a shovel in front surrounded by newspaper in order to get a draught, which then got the fire going.

Mondays were always set aside for washday. We had a dolly tub made of galvanized tin that was about three feet high and about twenty inches wide. We filled the tub with heated water from a tank built in at the side of the fireplace, and carried pans of water over to the dolly tub until there was enough to wash the clothes in. After sprinkling Persil into the water, we used a 'posser' – a round piece of metal, with holes to allow water through, attached to a wooden pole – to push down through the water so the clothes were continuously tossed about and the dirt squeezed out. It took about twenty minutes of hard work for each wash, and we usually had three washes in all.

We then had to put the clothes into a sink filled with cold water for rinsing. Once they were rinsed we had a mangle, which was basically two rollers (called wringers) with a turning handle at the side. The clothes were placed between the wringers so all the water could be squeezed out of them. They were then hung out to dry, or if the weather was bad, they were placed on a 'maiden' around the fire. Needless to say this was mainly in winter, so no one could get near the fire. This didn't go down well with any of us, but we had no other means of drying the clothes. There was an overhead rack on a pulley, but this was used to air the clothes that had been ironed.

The worst part of washday was the scrubbing board that was kept for clothes that were too dirty to go into the dolly tub. We had to get a block of Fairy washing soap and scrub the items until they came clean. My knuckles were red raw with the constant scrubbing. We always had to take a little scrubbing brush to father's collars. He didn't have shirts with collars: the collars were separate and fastened to the shirt with a stud at the back. This was so that he only had to change his work shirt once a week, putting on a fresh collar in-between. The collars had to be starched: that was a slimy affair. I didn't like washdays.

* * *

Because both my parents worked, my brother and I had to see to our own breakfasts and get ready for school. I didn't have any decent clothes or even a warm coat. I wore clogs that had irons on the bottom. This was so that we didn't have to keep buying new ones: we just had to change the irons. This meant that my feet hurt because they grew too big for the clogs.

I envied some of the girls at school because they had nice dresses and warm coats. But most of them were like me, except for the fact that I was very rebellious and was often to be found in the Headmaster's room, receiving ten strokes of the cane: five on each hand. My favourite subject at school was art. Maybe it was because I was good at it. I loved to draw – especially buildings – and I envisaged becoming an architect when I grew up.

During the week when my parents were working, Keith and I used to get up and see to ourselves. This meant getting our own breakfast, which usually consisted of bread and dripping in the winter, and bread and jam during the summer. This was if there *was* any bread; we often went to school hungry.

At lunchtime when the other children either had a packed lunch or had dinner tickets, I got into the habit of standing outside the toffee shop on the corner of the street that ran down the side of the school. I waited until someone went in and followed them inside. While the shopkeeper was distracted I pinched a bar of toffee off the counter. Or if I was lucky and there were bags of sweets that hadn't been sold, I picked a bag up, hid it under my coat and then sauntered out.

This went on for quite a while until one day I went in when there were quite a few people inside. I went over to look at some jars of toffee as I couldn't get to the counter, when suddenly a voice shouted, 'Oi, you! Stay where you are!'

My heart started thumping and I literally froze! The next thing I knew the shopkeeper swung me round, his angry face close to mine.

'You little thief, you've been pinching from my shop!'

'I haven't, Mister, honest. You can search me.'

'Search you,' he said, 'I've a mind to bring the police in! Go on, get out and don't come in here again!' With that he lashed out and smacked me one across the head.

I wasn't bothered about the smack, but I was embarrassed: all those people watching me. Thankfully no one knew me. If they had it would have got back to my parents; then I would have been in for it. Anyway, it frightened me that much, I preferred to go hungry from then on.

* * *

After school I usually met up with my best friend, Pat. Her father was a postman and for some reason I associated this with the fact that she always had sweets on her and sometimes leftover sandwiches that she shared with me.

She asked me if I wanted to go on the allotment or up to the daisy field. My general answer was, 'Well, I'm hungry, so let's go to the allotment.'

It was a very large allotment on which a number of men had garden patches. They grew vegetables, and apple and pear trees grew there so we had plenty of scope.

Looking back on it, I don't know why we bothered; we were always getting chased off. But apart from being hungry, they had the canes that they tied to the plants to make them grow straight and we needed these to make bows and arrows, which we were always breaking.

My brother Keith and his friend went into a shed nearby one day and found some ammunition and hand grenades. They were so naive that they took them to school, showing off as if they had won the war! This came to a sudden halt when the Headmaster got hold of them by their collars and marched them off to his office where they got a good caning.

Keith said to me recently, 'It's a wonder we didn't blow ourselves up, we were chucking them about like toys!'

* * *

The daisy field was a large field that ran the length between Pat's house and mine. We went there for two reasons: one being a large mound of earth that stretched over a stream. We jumped off the ledge over the stream and marked the place where we landed to see who went the furthest. This was a competition that we were both good at and used to challenge others to, especially if they had sweets on them.

The other reason we went there was because it had a tunnel the length of the daisy field that we could crawl through to the exit, which came out into the park. There we played on the swings and roundabout before going home for tea. We often missed school and spent all day in the park. It was situated in the next town and we knew about it walking home at teatime, because it took us at least an hour.

The truant officer was often at our house, eating cream cakes and drinking tea out of our best china cups, which Gwen kept for special occasions. She put on a posh voice, proclaiming innocence as to why I was absent from school so often, and why I was such a rebel. The truant officer always left fully assured that all was well at home and none the wiser as to the reasons for my behaviour. Had he stayed a while longer, he would have seen me running round the table trying to avoid the strap stinging my legs and making me dance.

* * *

We had to make our own entertainment. Ball games and skipping ropes played a major part of leisure time, and we had hoops that we used to roll with a stick. Playing marbles was a favourite game. A 'blood ally' was worth about four ordinary marbles. I always had a bag full because I was good at it.

My brother and I always got a shilling pocket money every Saturday, which is five pence in today's money. We went to the paper shop for a comic and sweets; then in the afternoon we went to the Regent Cinema for a matinee such as *Flash Gordon* and *The Three Stooges*. We also bought an ice-cream … all out of a shilling!

Chapter Three

MY FATHER HAD TWO JOBS. He worked in the mill during the day and collected money in the evenings for Relay, a cable network for wireless transmission. This was very popular because not many people had a television in those days. It was, however, very unfortunate for my brother and me because it presented the ideal situation for Gwen to use the strap. Human nature being what it is, she took to this new-found power and excelled in it.

The strap not only leaves an imprint on the body, it also leaves an imprint on the mind. This is why I remember so clearly the first time I found myself on the receiving end of it. I was sitting in the living room with my brother and Gwen; my father was out on his rounds, collecting money.

'There's two shillings missing out of my purse. Where is it?' Gwen asked. She had her purse in her hand.

'I don't know. Have you lost it?' I replied, not fully understanding what she meant.

I never saw it coming. One minute I was quietly sitting down; the next I was running screaming round the living room, trying to escape the blows that rained down on me.

When she had exhausted herself – I remember her trying to catch her breath – she said, 'That'll teach ya, get off to bed.'

I went to bed hurting all over and cried myself to sleep.

The following day I told my father what she had done and showed him the weal marks the strap had left on my legs. I don't know what she told him, but he concluded that I must have deserved it. I liked to think that he didn't really know. I was soon to find out otherwise.

* * *

My life took on a routine. Each evening when my father went out collecting, something went missing, or something out of the pantry was eaten without permission, and I was for it. I wasn't the only one; my brother also took a beating. I loved my brother very much and when I couldn't stand watching him crying and screaming any longer, I took the blame, knowing that she would turn on me and leave my brother alone. We were forbidden to eat any biscuits or drink any lemonade: Gwen counted the biscuits and marked the level of lemonade in the bottle. If any biscuits went missing or if the level mark dropped we were severely punished. We were leathered by our father countless times because of false accusations made by Gwen – as if we didn't have enough to put up with!

In truth, neither of us stole anything. We might have had some bread with jam on or a biscuit, but that was only because we were always hungry.

I eventually decided that if I was going to be punished so often and so cruelly regardless, then I might as well steal as much as I could and as often as I could. I went into the pantry and helped myself to tins of Nestlé cream milk. This was delicious; I spooned it out and savoured every mouthful. I got the Cadbury's cocoa tin and spooned some into a bag, then I added sugar and mixed it all up. I put my finger in my mouth to wet it, then stuck it into the mix and sucked it off. If there was no breakfast to be had, I took this to school with me and ate it along the way. Sometimes I took a whole tin of peaches, depending on how many there were on the shelf. Every weekend Gwen baked biscuits, jam tarts and buns, and I had a field day stealing these.

Keith and I also took other things from the house – like blankets and ornaments – and sold them to the second-hand shop in the centre of town. They must have made a vast profit out of the items as we only got pennies, no matter what we handed in. The lady in the shop must

10

have known they were stolen, but she took them all the same. I don't recall my parents ever getting anything back.

My father kept his collected Relay money in a bag that he kept in a glass cabinet in the front room. It had a lock on it, but I managed to undo it and fix it back so he wouldn't know. All the money in the bag consisted of shillings because that is what it cost each household for the use of the wireless. I pinched one or two shillings each week, and when he did his account books at the end of each week, I sat there holding my breath because I knew he would realise the money was missing, but he never said anything. I used to think he hadn't noticed, but he must have accepted that he had less to spend than he thought, rather than cause trouble for me. I like to think so anyway.

* * *

The worst times were when I went to bed. I lay there trying to stay awake, listening for the door at the bottom of the stairs. When I heard that click, I knew Gwen was coming up the stairs with the strap and I was ready for her. Sometimes I couldn't stay awake and she started on me before I could prepare myself. This was when it hurt the most. Even today, the slightest noise at night wakes me up.

I spent most of my childhood living in fear. I never wanted to go home and I stayed out after school playing with the other children. But when nightfall came and everyone had gone home I was left on my own and fear set into my heart. I was so afraid that sometimes I didn't go home; I went to the cemetery instead. I had found a large bush, which had enough room in the centre to curl up and go to sleep. Other times I stood outside our back gate, freezing cold, trying to pluck up the courage to go in. I became so tired that I was left with no choice; all I did was delay the punishment that awaited me.

I avoided home by going to my friend Pat's house and playing there. One evening I hid under her bed while she told her mother that I had gone home. After her mother had gone downstairs, I got into bed with Pat and we had a fine time whispering and giggling.

Eventually though, we heard noises outside. The police had come looking for me. I quickly hid under Pat's bed again; just in time before her mother came in and asked if she knew where I was. When her mother had gone back downstairs again, we both got scared and I decided to climb out of the bedroom window. I was halfway down the drainpipe when the police shone a torch on me. I was taken back home by the police, and when they left I got a good hiding.

* * *

Gwen gave us a list of chores to do each day. We had to clean the cutlery using Silvo to polish each item, after which they had to be washed in soapy water. We also had to polish the lino on the flagged floor, and if it wasn't spotless we had to do it again and again until it shone.

I had to spend Saturday mornings baking. The flour and lard had to be mixed to perfection: if Gwen saw a single crumb in it I would get hit. My fingers ached, but I didn't dare stop until she said, for fear of getting another thump. Sometimes she hit me so hard it knocked me to the floor. I always did my best not to cry as I'd discovered that when I cried she used it as another excuse to lay into me.

A particularly hated chore was massaging Gwen's scalp with oil because her hair was very thin. Both Keith and I had to spend hours doing this. It didn't matter if our hands hurt; we daren't stop. What's more, our work was all in vain. Her hair never grew: later on in life she wore a wig.

* * *

Evacuees were housed in our area because the war was on. One of them – a lad called Dennis – set our pantry on fire. We tried to put it out with towels, but it took hold and by the time we had managed to put it out everything was black, including my brother and me. All hell let loose that night. Keith and I had to take the blame because Dennis shouldn't have been let in – it was a strict rule that no one was allowed in – so we received a beating for something we hadn't done. We didn't get a chance to let anyone in again: Gwen took the door key from Keith and we were locked out.

* * *

I don't recall ever being happy and I never knew the love of a parent, but my brother looked after me. There was only one other girl who lived near us and she never used to play out, so I went everywhere with Keith and his friends. There was a railway siding at the bottom of our street and we used to play inside the carriages. I was always climbing on roofs, jumping into coal stacks, playing football and fighting.

There were two markets in Nelson. One was the open market that sold fresh meat, flowers and vegetables. The other was a closed market and because it had a roof it was busier and more popular, with a larger variety of goods on sale. One of the stalls in the closed market was a toffee stall that was run by my Aunty Margaret's friend, Alice. She sold a variety of toffee: plain, nut and fudge. She laid them out in trays and broke them up with her little toffee hammer, and then served it in two-ounce and four-ounce bags.

Sometimes she let me and Keith scrape the trays when they were done with, but we had a secret supply of this toffee. One day when we were playing out we noticed a van pull up outside a building.

Keith said, 'That's got "Fergus Taylor" written on the side.'

'It's the toffee makers who Alice buys her toffee trays from,' I said. 'Let's go and investigate.'

We opened the door of the building and peered inside. What a sight! And what a smell! There were three cauldrons in a row filled with toffee and a man walked along stirring each one with what I thought was a big paddle. The smell was so wonderfully delicious I thought I had opened the door to heaven. Then the man saw us.

'Well! What are you two doing in here?'

'We saw the van pull up,' I replied.

'So you thought you'd come and have a look in, did you?' he said.

'My Aunty's friend sells your toffee on a stall.'

13

'Right then, you better start scraping them trays clean and when you're done you can wash 'em out for me.'

And so began our friendship with this lovely man. He supplied us with toffee bags that we filled and sold to classmates at four pennies a quarter. We built up quite a little business. He never allowed any other children to come in and I know now that he felt sorry for us.

* * *

My father was a long-standing member of the Old Band Club that was situated at the top of our street. One year they hired a coach to take all the children to Southport for the day. Keith and I showed up, all excited, along with the other children. We were given sweets and five shillings to spend on the fairground. Just as we were about to board the coach, we were told that we couldn't go because our father was no longer a member.

They then had a long discussion while Keith and I stood on the pavement waiting, and eventually decided that we could go after all. I don't know why they changed their minds: I think it was because they felt sorry for us. My father hadn't realised that they had struck him off the register because he hadn't been attending meetings or been drinking there: Gwen put a stop to that as soon as she married him.

* * *

Gwen's brother Tom lived in the end house on our street. He never had anything to do with her, but he and his wife were kind to Keith and me. They had two boys, Tom and Alan, who we played out with, and they always came with presents for us at Christmas. One year we got a Waddington Monopoly board. I thought it was a rich relative as it had the same surname as me! When Gwen and Tom's mother was dying in our front room, she said to Gwen, 'Be good to those children, Gwen.'

Tom and his mother were two people who knew what Gwen was like: it's a pity they never had a voice.

May Day was always a wonderful day. The May Queen led the

14

procession, followed by children from the different churches. Those who couldn't walk – young and old – rode on the carts, which were decorated with ribbons, balloons and flowers. Everyone entered into the procession. Massey's Brewery had decorated carthorses, and there were milk floats, coal floats and butchers' and bakers' vans. People lined the streets with their chairs all along the route. It was one day in the year when everyone was happy.

Other than these brief encounters of happiness, it was a most miserable life. My Aunty Margaret must have known what was going on, but although she was always good to us, she never did anything by way of rescuing us.

Keith used to run away a lot. He had a bicycle and stayed away from home for days. I once asked him where he had been and he said he had cycled to Blackpool, which was about thirty miles away. He said he had slept on the ghost train and then early one morning the police had caught him. He told them he was on the street so early because he had a paper round, but they didn't believe him because he was filthy with dirt. Father had to go and pick him up from the police station. When he came home he got a good thrashing.

Although neighbours complained to the police about the screaming they regularly heard, no one believed us; mainly because in those days children had few rights and they certainly had no say. 'Children should be seen and not heard' was often said. I remember speaking once at the table during dinner and was knocked off my chair to the floor for it. I wasn't allowed back to the table either.

One time Gwen was standing on the mat by the sink cleaning the windows, when the mat slipped and she fell backwards. She lay on the floor with her eyes closed, while Keith and I just looked at her, mesmerised. I don't know what Keith thought, but I know to this day that I willed her not to get up and hoped she was dead. We had suffered so much at the hands of this woman. My heart sank when she opened her eyes and got up; no worse for the fall. No reprieve for us children: life carried on as normal.

* * *

I was once taken ill with scarlet fever and was in bed for a few days. I was unable to swallow, but all Gwen brought me were two ginger biscuits. My Aunty Margaret came round, took one look at me, and immediately called the doctor.

I was taken to Reedyford Hospital and given an enema. A funnel was inserted and hot soapy water poured through it into my bowels. After that I had to keep running to the toilet.

When Aunty Margaret visited me while I was on the children's ward, she brought me a big bottle of Sasparilla, but as soon as she left the nurse took it away. I caused a rumpus over that, but it was procedure that everything was handed in and then shared among all the children.

The hospital was later demolished, which I thought was a shame because it was built for the people of Nelson and paid for by the workers who contributed a shilling a week out of their wages.

* * *

I was a child and I only thought as a child. Gwen had all the attributes of a grown woman: she was clever, knowledgeable and wise in many ways … and she was very devious. No one in the family knew what was going on – or they didn't want to know – except for my Aunty Ivy.

My father had two sisters: my Aunty Margaret – a big woman who did her best by way of giving us treats and occasionally feeding us – and Aunty Ivy, who was small and thin. They didn't look like sisters.

I remember an incident that took place at Hilldrop. I don't know why it's called Hilldrop, but it's a hill that drops at the bottom and runs across the bottom of Earl Street where we lived. I was walking down the hill with Gwen when I saw Aunty Ivy coming towards us. She lived in the next town so I thought she must be going to our house.

Not only was she on her way to see us, but she was blazing mad. I don't recall the exact words that were exchanged, but she told Gwen to leave us children alone, that she knew what was going on and that she was going to put the police onto her. Gwen denied it all, but then Aunty Ivy smacked her across the face and walked off.

'Yes!' I thought. I could have jumped with joy, but I had to pretend that I felt sorry for her. For the first time since Gwen had come into our lives I thought things might change, but by a strange twist of fate, it was not to be.

I think I must have been about eleven years old, which would make it 1946. A flu epidemic called the Asian Flu spread through Lancashire. My Aunty Ivy caught the flu and died within the week. I believe she was the first of many who were taken with this epidemic, and all my hopes were dashed. Had she lived, my life would in all probability have taken a different course.

* * *

Gwen had an ally in my Granddad Nutter, my mother's father. He always encouraged her to discipline us, although I don't think he knew the extent to which she administered the so-called discipline.

I was present with Gwen when he was on his deathbed. He said to her, 'I think we were wrong about these children.' It's a pity that it took him so long to realise this.

Years later, when I was in the army, Granddad Nutter's housekeeper wrote to me. She explained she was not well and that Gwen had offered to look after her on the condition she left certain items in her will to Gwen. The housekeeper asked my advice. I told her to agree, but to actually leave her nothing. I found out later Gwen had searched the house from top to bottom looking for the will. As a last resort, she took all the coal out of the bunker and had my father and Keith carry it to our house.

* * *

I don't recall getting birthday presents, but at Christmas I always got a stocking at the bottom of the bed. Inside the stocking was an apple, an orange, some nuts and a few sweets. On one rare occasion I got a doll; she had no clothes and only had one eye, but she became my close companion.

The only book I ever received was my Sunday School prize book. I got a ticket – the value of which related to our attendance at Sunday School – and I took the ticket to Gerard's bookshop in the centre of Nelson and chose a book. I hated having to leave the book in the shop and didn't get to see it again until prize-giving day at the church.

* * *

My life at the end of a strap was coming to an end. One night when I was in bed, Gwen came in and raised the strap, but as it came down I grabbed her wrist. She shouted at me to let go, but I held on. She never raised that strap to me again. I was twelve years old and I thought I had gained a victory. Little did I know that she was planning to get rid of me.

Although things quietened down with the strap, the accusations continued: some true and some false. Gwen devised different methods of dealing with me. Every Friday evening we went to Aunty Margaret's. It was the highlight of the week; we always had pie and peas and cream buns for afters. Gwen waited until just before we were due to go, then she told me I couldn't go. I had to use all the control I could muster not to cry.

Eventually, Gwen succeeded. She sent me away to an approved school in Coventry.

Chapter Four

NEWFIELD SCHOOL WAS AN APPROVED school for girls. Those who were sent there had usually broken the law in some form or other and the punishment was to be sent away from home and be taught how to become responsible citizens.

When I arrived at the school I was terrified. I had left home crying and had endured a long journey with strangers, not knowing where I was going, how long I was going for, or if I would ever return home. Nobody had told me anything, other than I was a bad girl and was being sent away.

The school was a large imposing building, set in its own grounds, with a lodge at the bottom of the driveway. It must have belonged to some rich land owner at some time. This great house was to become my home for the next two years.

There were about sixty or more girls accommodated in the dormitories. There was a kitchen, dining room, assembly room, sewing room, boardroom and staffroom. The Headmistress had her own room and she lived in the lodge at the bottom of the drive.

My arrival at Newfield was one of the most momentous days of my young life. I needn't have been frightened; it was like entering a whole new way of life. I didn't know there could be such happiness, never having been very happy, or very far from the strap. I truly couldn't believe such a wonderful life existed and I was to be part of it: it was a new beginning.

On my arrival I was given a new set of clothes, which included, wonder of wonders, some new shoes. I felt very smart and, more importantly, for the first time in my life, I felt that someone cared. I was given a meal and went off to bed with my new nightdress and slippers. There were six beds in my dormitory. The girls must have been told about a new arrival because they were all awake and had a barrage of questions for me.

The following morning I went to assembly where we had roll-call and prayers. This was followed by breakfast, after which the other girls went off to school. I was shown round the building and introduced to all the staff, and the Headmistress explained all the rules and regulations. She said that she hoped I would be happy there, and by the smile on my face, that was very likely.

At the time of my arrival, the Headmistress was about to leave. This was because when her son came home on leave during school holidays, even though he resided at the lodge, he caused quite a stir amongst the girls. This was not felt to be appropriate.

The new headmistress was called Miss Brady. To say that Miss Brady was unique, I believe, would be an understatement. She combined discipline and authority with kindness and compassion. She was a shining example to us all and she loved us all equally.

It is therefore no wonder that the school ran so efficiently. All the staff, including Miss Brady, were ex-army officers, with the exception of Miss Morton, the sewing mistress. I was to become one of Miss Morton's favourites and spent many happy hours in her sewing room mending socks, making dresses and repairing uniforms. She was the kind of person who said that she had no favourites, all the while making me feel special.

We were sent out to different schools in Coventry, and I attended Frederick Bird Secondary Modern School. I think it was a case of whether a person was Church of England or Roman Catholic as to which school they attended. When I set off on my first day I had a brand new uniform on and I was very proud of it, almost to the point of swaggering. I was fortunate in so much as several of the girls from Newfield attended this school, so I slipped in unnoticed.

I got along well with the girls at school. Had they known I came from an approved school and not a boarding school, it might have been a different story. I can't say that I envied them because they returned home, but I do remember feeling twinges of sadness at the absence of my own family life when they chatted about parties, going to the pictures and boyfriends. But in the main I was content and just thought of them as being spoilt.

I did well in all my lessons, so much so that Miss Brady sent me and one other pupil to night school to learn shorthand and typing. We went two evenings a week, but I didn't like shorthand, mainly because of a lack of interest. I recall Miss Brady being disappointed. She had to accept that I wasn't as clever as she thought I was. I regretted not putting more effort into it later on.

* * *

There was a group of girls in Newfield School that were bad, and I mean bad. There were around eight of them with a leader called Beryl, and they picked on the weaker ones. They took sweets off them, mimicked them and, worst of all, hit and kicked them. One day Beryl and her gang surrounded me in the corridor. She started taking the mickey and the rest of them joined in, so I punched her in the stomach, and then smacked her in the face. I asked the others if they wanted some and they all backed off.

Word must have got around and from then on I became a leader. It felt good because I was able to protect the weaker ones. I was no angel, though. I used to raid the food store and hold midnight feasts in the dormitory. I sneaked out at night to meet up with the choirboys from the church. They were harmless activities that I did out of a sense of adventure.

The police didn't think it was harmless, though, when my friend and I absconded. We pinched two bikes and headed for London. We had reached Rugby before they caught us, and put us in a cell while we awaited transport back to the school. All our privileges were stopped; we were caned, and made to stand in front of everyone at assembly next day while Miss Brady gave us a good ticking off. What I learnt from this incident was that I had not only let myself down, but also the school. But in the eyes of the other girls my friend and I were heroes.

It wasn't long after this incident that we were told at evening assembly the board had decided certain children were found to be unsuitable for Newfield and they were to be moved the following morning to a new school.

I got no sleep that night and I never prayed so much in my life. For the first time since my arrival, I was frightened; in fact I was scared stiff. I didn't want to leave Newfield and go into the unknown. I promised God that I would never do anything wrong again.

The following day, as time went on, I slowly began to realise that certain girls were missing. Beryl and her gang were all gone. I found out later that they were all taken out while the rest of us were asleep. I think the whole school was relieved and I felt as though I had been given a second chance.

When I told Miss Brady that I thought I might have been one of them to go, she said, 'No, Doreen, you were never bad.' I knew where she was coming from.

A few weeks before this incident, Miss Brady called me into her office and handed me a letter from my father. All letters were read by a member of staff prior to our receiving them. In the letter he said he knew my stepmother had instigated my removal from home, that I had been accused of things I had not done, and he was sorry he had not stood up for me. He said that if I wanted to do something about it he would stand by me. He also added that Gwen was trying to get rid of him. I wondered if he would have acknowledged any of this had she not been.

Miss Brady asked me if I wanted to do anything about it, and told me that as far as she was concerned, I should not be in an approved school. She said the board could look into it on my behalf.

'No,' I said. 'I don't want to cause any trouble.' I felt that I'd had enough trouble in my life and I was happy to remain at Newfield.

* * *

Doreen Salmon

I went home once during my time at the school. While I was at home no incidents occurred; I think that was because Gwen knew I was going back to school. The most vivid memory I have of this leave was of an infection I got down the side of my thumb. It was caused by a 'wicklow' (where the 'wick', down the side of a thumb or finger, is sufficiently low enough to allow an infection to set in). I don't think they are as common these days. It caused me lots of pain. I recall one of my aunts coming to the house and she stuck my thumb in a basin of scalding hot water. I ended up having to have the wicklow lanced, which got rid of the pain and left me with a scar that remains to this day. I was still in pain when travelling back to school on the train. There was a man in the same carriage who was very sympathetic. He was from Malta and said he was a director at Courtalls Silk Manufacturers. He gave me his business card and said if he could ever do anything for me I was to contact him. I gave the card to Miss Brady who said it was very nice of him, but I think she thought differently.

* * *

When I lived at home, before being sent to Newfield, I had attended Woodland Road Baptist Church, where we were instructed on religious matters. As a result of this I was baptised. However, while I was at Newfield I attended a Church of England church. We set off every Sunday morning; Catholics in one direction and the rest of us in the other. I was encouraged to attend confirmation classes, which I did, but for all the wrong reasons. Firstly, I wanted to please Miss Brady. Secondly, it meant that I could go out at night as the lessons were held in the evening. And thirdly, I could meet up with boys.

I eventually became a confirmed member of the Church of England. As I understood it, Jesus was born in a stable. I felt very sympathetic towards him. I understood him to be a very good man who worked many miracles and died for me so that I could become like him. I was all for it. It wasn't until later on in life that I became aware of the true significance of the life of Jesus. Suffice to say, at the tender age of fourteen, I had been both baptised and confirmed.

ONE OF A KIND

* * *

When the time came for me to leave Newfield I was very upset. I had known great love and understanding from all the staff, and in particular Miss Brady. Who would have thought that such a school existed in those times, but exist it did, and there are many other girls who benefited alongside me. We had a lot to be grateful for.

On my last evening I cried. We always assembled for evening prayer and closed with a hymn. That evening we sang 'How Great Thou Art'. It was all too much for me and I burst into tears.

The following morning I dressed up in a new outfit that I had chosen myself. I said goodbye to everyone, promised to be good, and not to forget them. How could I? I left with one thought in my mind and that was as soon as I was old enough I was going to join the army.

I arrived home with mixed feelings. I was glad to be home, but the future seemed uncertain. I was especially glad to see my father. I had always loved him, despite his shortcomings. Gwen, I was uncertain about. I think I had been home for about three days when she came downstairs and said, 'There's ten shillings missing out of my purse.'

I didn't answer her. I just put my coat on and went looking for my father, who was still out collecting for Relay. He came back home with me and he gave her a tongue-lashing – the likes of which I had never heard before – including the threat of a good hiding and calling in the police. Well, that was that; she never accused me again and it brought to a close the brutality I had suffered at her hands.

Chapter Five

NOTHING OF GREAT SIGNIFICANCE TOOK place over the next eighteen months. I went to work as a clerk at our local newspaper, the *Nelson Leader*, using my typing skills. I also went on holiday to Southport. I went to the fairground and on a ride that made me sick. My father had given me ten shillings, which was a lot of money in those days. I went on the promenade and a man with a camera took my photograph, and my ten shillings along with it.

I also went ballroom dancing down at the Imperial and learnt to dance, which I really enjoyed. The boys stood on one side of the room and the girls sat on the other side. We spent all evening dancing with each other, until the last dance when the boys dashed across the dance floor and made a beeline for the girl of their choice. If we were lucky one of them walked us home; we were even luckier if we got a kiss.

* * *

Eventually the day arrived. I was seventeen and a half; the exact age for becoming eligible to join the army. I went to the recruiting office in Manchester and had a medical examination and written tests. I passed with flying colours. I was told to go back home and wait to hear from them. I was very excited and couldn't wait.

I remember coming home from work each evening expecting a letter. It took them about ten days, but finally I had it in my hands.

You have been accepted as a recruit in Her Majesty's Services the Women's Royal Army Corps

I was to report for training to Guildford about a week later.

Gwen told me that before I could join the army I had to agree to send five shillings a week home, because they couldn't manage without my wage. This was nonsense; they had managed perfectly well before. She once more had the upper hand because at that time children were not allowed to leave home without their parents' consent. To be honest, I would have agreed to anything. As it turned out I only got seven and sixpence a week, so I had very little left as we had to buy all our own toiletries and cleaning materials. I stuck to my promise, though, and arranged for the paymaster to send five shillings home every week.

When I set off by train to Guildford a week later for my training, it seemed to take forever to get there, but I was extremely excited. I arrived around teatime. I had a shower, a haircut and was inspected for nits; then I was issued with my uniform. I was as proud as a peacock. I had achieved my ambition; at long last I was in the army. I thought that by joining up I would become like the staff at Newfield School. I was very naive.

I slept in the barracks with about sixteen other girls, all of whom had arrived that day from different walks of life. Reveille – a signal sounded to wake us up – the next morning was a bit of a shocker. I wasn't used to getting up at six o clock. I put on my new uniform, even though there had been no time to press it. Breakfast was self-service so I made a pig of myself. I was so hungry I could have eaten twice. When we returned to the barracks we were shown how to make our beds, which was very complicated. We were also shown how to press our uniform, shirt, battledress and skirt. When we saw the razor-edge creases in the Sergeant's uniform we knew we had a long way to go.

We then assembled outside on the parade ground. This is when I realised that some of the girls didn't have berets. They obviously had nits. I felt sorry for them; they must have come from poor families. I must admit, I didn't make friends with them; not because they had nits, but because they kept to themselves, which was understandable. I didn't get on with them because they gave us dirty looks if we spoke to them, so they obviously didn't want to be friendly with the rest of us.

We had to learn how to march. I loved marching. I strode out, keeping in step of course, with my head up in the air, feeling very important. We drilled for hours: there was always someone out of step or going the wrong way, but we got it right in the end. Most of our time was taken up with kit inspections, drilling, cleaning, pressing uniforms and bulling shoes. We also had to attend various lessons, mainly about army life. We had six weeks of training in total before our passing-out parade.

Prior to passing out we all had to go for an interview to decide which regiment we were to join. I had considered the different options and, as I didn't know what most of them entailed, I decided I would settle for whatever they suggested, with the exception of the catering corps; I hated cooking. In the end I was allocated to the Anti-Aircraft Command, with which I was very satisfied.

When the day arrived it was very exciting. Everyone looked smart and I for one felt as though I had achieved something positive and worthwhile in my life.

I had written to Miss Brady to ask her to come and when she arrived we had a good talk, along with tea and buns. She said she was very proud of me.

When it came to the parade we all had to salute the commanding officer on the stand. I saw Miss Brady there amongst the officers, and I in turn was very proud of her.

* * *

I said goodbye to Guildford and my friends and we all went our separate ways. My posting was to Ack Ack Command, Lingfield, in Surrey, so I didn't have far to travel.

I soon settled into the routine of army life. I worked in the plotting room where I learnt to plot aircraft. It was interesting work. We went to firing camp twice a year, where we plotted aircraft coming in and phoned through the coordinates so the gunners were able to set the guns ready to fire. They didn't fire at the aircraft; they fired at the sleeves which flew some distance behind the aircraft. I don't think they hit them very often, but it was dangerous. I remember one lad had his finger chopped off because he was not quick enough putting the shell in.

I became engaged while stationed at Lingfield. His name was Peter Bampton and he was known as 'Chick'. I'd never had a boyfriend, but this lad really caught my eye and I did all I could to catch his eye. He was very handsome and very athletic. Each week he went to the swimming baths. I went to the length of buying a two-piece bathing costume and went swimming the same evening he did. I waited until he looked over and then did a very graceful dive into the deep end. I came up minus the bottom half and had to go back under water to retrieve it. Regardless of this incident, I did eventually get his attention and it wasn't long before we were engaged.

About a year later I returned from leave and found out he had been going out with a cook who I knew had been doing her best to take him off me. He tried to explain it to me, but I wouldn't listen. I had half expected it to happen, so I broke off the engagement.

The only other romance I had after that was with an officer. Other ranks and officers were not allowed to mix, but this particular officer had been eyeing me up for quite some time. The girls were forever encouraging me to go out on a date with him, so when he asked me out I said yes. It was the most boring evening ever. He was self-opinionated and a complete snob. When he brought me back to barracks he gave me a big sloppy kiss and I never went out with him again.

* * *

On my days off my friend and I went out in our uniforms and hung about at the barracks gate. We often got a lift into Brighton or Eastbourne. On one occasion two Polish bikers stopped. They were riding Black Vincents, and offered us lifts to Eastbourne.

When we set off on what was quite a long journey, I thought my breakfast was on its way up! I knew for certain we would be there within an hour. We spent the day sunbathing on the front, and had sandwiches and ice cream, which the bikers refused to let us pay for. We had the same fast journey home, where they dropped us off at the barracks. Not even a kiss; they were perfect gentlemen.

We used to get weekend passes and sometimes a seventy-two hour pass. I set off hitchhiking. I always took a friend with me, even though it was quite safe to hitchhike in those days. We made for the A1, which was the main road leading north – there were no motorways then. We always travelled with lorry drivers, spent a day at home, and then set off back. On one occasion there was a police roadblock and we were not able to get through. We arrived back at camp twelve hours late. We were put on a charge, confined to barracks for four weeks and had one week's loss of pay.

* * *

I remained at Lingfield for two years before I decided I needed a change, so I put in an application to become a training Non-Commissioned Officer (NCO). My application was accepted and I returned to Guildford where I received my first stripe and became an NCO. I was now the one with the smart uniform and the new recruits looked at me the same way I had looked at the NCOs on my first arrival.

I soon settled into life as a training NCO. I had my own room at the end of the barrack room and a bunch of new friends. We went into Guildford on our days off, usually to the cinema and a meal afterwards. We didn't mix with the other ranks in the same way that the officers didn't mix with us.

I received full pay as an NCO and I decided after two years that I had contributed enough money to home. My father and Gwen never made any reference to the money when I received letters from them; which were few and far between anyway.

Because I had sufficient funds I decided to go to Newfield School for a weekend visit. It was really nice seeing all the staff again. I enjoyed my stay, but it wasn't the same. I didn't know any of the girls and, although the staff made me welcome, I think it was a mistake. I returned to barracks and I never came across anyone from Newfield again, but I will never forget my time spent there or the love and the care that was given to me by them.

* * *

I enlisted in the army for three years. Towards the end of the third year I was admitted to hospital with appendicitis. The hospital was run by the Queen Alexandra Royal Nursing Corps. While I was there it was announced that the Queen Mother was to pay a visit. When the day arrived we were all told to stand at the bottom of our beds and we had to curtsy. There was a lot of hustle and bustle, and everything had to be spotless. When the Queen Mother walked down the ward we all stood with 'eyes front'. When she stopped in front of me, matron said, 'This is Corporal Waddington, Ma'am.'

'And how long have you been in, Corporal?' asked the Queen Mother.

'Three years, Ma'am,' I replied.

'You poor dear.'

Matron gave me a funny look, and I realised the Queen Mother had meant how long had I been in hospital, not the army!

* * *

At the end of my three years I decided to leave the army and try my luck in Civvy Street. I went to live in Skegness. I liked the idea of living by the sea and I had an ex-army friend who lived there. I found myself some lodgings with an elderly lady whose son was a police inspector. I also found myself two jobs. I worked in a factory where they made radios, and I worked as a waitress in a local restaurant at the weekends. I loved this job. I was put on 'the Burma Road', so named because it was a long way from the kitchen, but I didn't mind. The best part was the tips. It was very busy in the summer and I earned lots of money.

Doreen Salmon

Summer was great, but winter was miserable, and I missed the community-style way of living, so I decided to re-enlist. This time I was more ambitious; I wanted to join the Military Police, better known as the Red Caps.

It wasn't as easy as I thought it would be to get into the Military Police. I had to take some very hard exams, and I wasn't sure if I had done well enough to pass. I also had to give a fifteen-minute lecture: mine was about outer space. Even when I was finally accepted, I had to go on probation for a few months.

I had to go out on patrol with another seasoned NCO to learn how to deal with other ranks. We had authority over ranks higher than ourselves so we had to be very professional. The hardest part of the training was learning the law. There was so much to learn; we even went to Bow Street Court to watch the proceedings there. Eventually I got through and became a fully fledged Red Cap.

We patrolled mainly in London in a Land Rover. If we saw army personnel behaving badly or not properly dressed we spoke to them, and if they responded politely we just sent them on their way. They were not usually polite and we had to arrest them. I tried to avoid this if at all possible because it meant a load of paperwork. If the charge was serious I sometimes had to attend a court martial. I was on holiday on the Norfolk Broads one year when I was summoned back to camp to attend one. I remember it well because I had a really bad toothache and I thought I'd be able to visit the dentist, which I did, but he didn't take the tooth out and I returned to my holiday still in pain.

The Private, whose court martial it was, had previously been arrested in Woolwich. I was on patrol with a lance corporal. We always went in twos in order to have a witness to corroborate any incidents in which we might be involved. On this occasion a group of WRAC personnel were exiting a public house and one of the women was not properly dressed. Her battledress was undone and she hadn't put on her beret. I approached her.

'Put your beret on and do up your jacket,' I said.

'Oh yes, and what are you going to do about it?' she replied.

'If you don't do as you're told, I shall arrest you.'

By this time a crowd had gathered and we found ourselves surrounded by a number of uniformed army and navy men and women who became hostile, both verbally and physically. I realised we were in trouble, but fortunately the civilian police arrived in a large black van. They dispersed the crowd and, while they were doing so, the Private who I had approached took a swing at me, knocking off my cap. A police officer caught hold of her, marched her off to the van and threw her inside. We finished up at the local police station where she was handed over to our custody and later charged with disobeying an order and assault.

On the day of her trial the Lance Corporal was called in to give evidence first while I waited outside. They didn't end up calling me in because when the Lance Corporal started to give her evidence, the Private said, 'You're a f***ing liar,' and knocked the Lance Corporal to the ground. She was immediately dishonourably discharged from the army.

* * *

I was always hungry and, although I went to all the meals at the cookhouse, I spent a good deal of my pay at the Navy, Army, and Air Force Institutes (NAAFI), which was run by civilians for the Armed Forces. Sandwiches and cream cakes could be bought there. We generally had a good time at the NAAFI, especially when special events were organised like table tennis competitions and dances.

I had a friend called Sheila, who came from Fleetwood, and had joined around the same time as me. We decided to buy a scooter together, mainly to drive round Richmond Park, but I didn't take to it. Having never owned a bicycle, never mind a scooter, I wasn't able to balance so I kept coming off and gave it up as a bad job.

We had a perimeter round our camp with gates that we kept locked at night. When I was on duty one evening a man delivered a parcel that was addressed to the Staff Sergeant. I took delivery of it and passed it on: it was a pair of incontinence knickers that our 'practical joker' had ordered for her.

Doreen Salmon

One day I was in the bath and the practical joker climbed up the partition and poured some powder into the water. When I stood up, my lower half was blue. She was always up to something but we couldn't really do anything about it.

* * *

I was very good at netball and went regularly to the gym to practise. I eventually got picked for the team and we went on to the finals of the South Region Championships. We didn't win, but we were presented with a runner-up medal by the Duchess of Kent. I did have a photo of the event, but lost it on my travels.

The other sport I was good at was rifle shooting. I went in my spare time to where the men practised indoors with .22 rifles. I also went outdoors on 'the butts'. I don't know what the word meant, but we shot .303 rifles at targets in the butts, which were about two hundred yards away. A man signalled the score by means of a long pole with a round marker attached to the end. I enjoyed this and became quite a markswoman.

The camp where I was stationed was in Richmond Park. It could not have been more perfect: it was a beautiful park where the deer roamed free. I often drove around; it was such a pleasure. The town of Kingston-upon-Thames was different altogether to where I was brought up. It had much posher and nicer shops. I liked living there.

We were sent on duty to Earl's Court for the Royal Tournament. I had been there before in an exhibition. There were fifty girls from each service: Navy, Army and Air Force. We performed a dance with hoops, but unfortunately we followed the horse display, so the ground beneath our feet caused us to stumble. I wrote to my Aunty Margaret to tell her about it because it was being televised. She told me later that she just picked me out when the camera moved away from me.

The reason we were on duty at Earl's Court was because everywhere that royalty went, we went. On this occasion I was guard of honour to the Queen, Prince Philip and Princess Margaret. I was surprised at how small the Queen and the Princess were, and I thought that Prince Philip needed a haircut.

We were told that when the ceremony ended we were to report to one of the rooms upstairs because King Hussein of Jordan had asked to meet us. I was very surprised by this as it was most unusual for royalty to ask to speak with us. There were five of us: a sergeant, two corporals and two lance corporals. We all assembled in the allotted room and lined up ready to salute the King. He was a very pleasant person; he shook hands with us all and informed us that he was looking for a bride. As it happens he didn't find one that day, but I was informed some time later that he had married a British nurse. Good on him.

* * *

The camp itself was well run, mainly by the Sergeant Major. I got on very well with all the people stationed there; that is, until about eight girls returned to camp after serving in Cyprus. They didn't want to mix with us; they had longer time in service than us and always came 'the old soldier'. We couldn't do much about it because they were not actually bullying us, just making our lives uncomfortable. Eventually I went to see the Regimental Sergeant Major (RSM) with the intention of telling her what was going on. She already knew and told me not to worry as she was dealing with it. I don't know what she did, but things improved and we all started getting on together.

I was posted to Catterick for a short term. It wasn't anywhere near as good as Kingston. I didn't like it there; it always seemed to be raining. I was put on school crossings, which I didn't mind because it gave me the opportunity to control traffic. I took great pleasure in this: I had the power to make traffic stop and I loved it. I also learnt to drive while there. I had to learn to reverse first as I had to back out from my billet. I learnt to drive in the dark too as the Staff Sergeant was teaching me in her own time, so we had to go after duty hours. I passed my test first time.

While stationed at Catterick I went home on leave with a friend. It being nearer home than London, it wasn't so long a journey. We also went to Blackpool and the Lake District for days out; then I hired a car and, unbelievably, we went to London. I think I had got used to the south; there was so much more going on. Besides which, having just passed my test, I wanted to drive. I remember having a near miss on the way down; otherwise we enjoyed our trip and returned to camp on time.

Before leaving Catterick, I was put on special duties at an army barracks where there was a passing-out parade. I and one other had to attend because the Duke of Kent and his bride-to-be were in attendance. I wasn't very impressed by this royal person, but the young lady was very gracious and pretty.

My time at Catterick at an end, I returned to Kingston and was promoted to full Corporal which meant I then had two stripes.

* * *

I soon settled back into the routine, and most of my time was taken up with patrols. We often travelled by train into London, mainly because we covered the railway stations, working alongside the railway police. On one occasion the train was packed with businessmen and one gentleman put his bowler hat on the seat next to him. The Lance Corporal who was with me put some mints into the hat. I gave her fierce looks to take them out. She did eventually and threw them out of the window, but they came flying back in and hit her in the face. She was called Sharmaine, but we called her Bimbo. She was the corps practical joker.

I went on special duties many times while stationed at Kingston. I never enjoyed it when we were on Horse Guards Parade; we stood for up to two hours before the Queen put in an appearance. Some of the soldiers fainted and that meant an automatic charge. I don't think the Queen was aware of this; I suppose she was too busy keeping to her schedule.

I enjoyed the Trooping of the Colour. I never took part in it because we were always placed at the road's edge, near The Cenotaph. I loved all the marching, seeing all the regiments, old and new, and listening to the bands. We used to watch out for those who were out of step. It struck me as funny the way they used to shuffle, doing their best to get back in step. Overall it was a momentous occasion and made us appreciate all that the Armed Forces did for their country.

* * *

I wasn't back at Kingston long before I was told I was being posted to Cyprus. I was given my jabs and told to scrub some floors; this was to get the circulation going. I fainted and woke up in the sickbay. I soon recovered and was sitting up in bed, eating a sausage sandwich, when the duty officer came round.

I was very excited. I was issued with an overseas kit and taken to a military airbase where I was to fly to Cyprus, where the Greek Cypriots were fighting the Turkish Cypriots. I was off to war.

The flight to Cyprus involved a stopover at Athens, which was very hot, but landing at Nicosia airport mid-afternoon and being ferried onto a three-tonne open lorry was literally breathtaking. The heat when travelling blew hot air into my lungs and the dust that was thrown up from the sandy sun-baked roads made the journey one I would not soon forget. We travelled from Nicosia to Episkopi – which was from one end of the island to the other – which took about two hours. There is now a motorway that runs from one end of the island to the other and it takes less than an hour, but fifty years ago there were no such luxuries.

We arrived at camp looking and feeling weary and dejected. On arrival we were told to shower right away as we were overdue and the RSM was waiting. No one seemed the least bit interested in our pleas for food and drink, although we were given a drink of orange squash prior to the meeting.

There were six of us in all and the meeting lasted about forty minutes. We were told what duties were to be carried out: 7 a.m. until noon was patrolling the camp area; noon until 5 p.m. we were off duty; and 7 p.m. until 11 p.m. we were back on duty patrolling the camp area; with alternate weekends off. We were told we had to be vigilant, patrolling the camp perimeter, looking out for any intruders, suspicious items or anyone acting strangely (as in running away, having planted a bomb). We were duly dismissed and we made a beeline for the canteen.

We were shown round the camp the following morning. It was situated in a valley called Happy Valley, which was strange because my hometown of Nelson also has a Happy Valley, situated between Nelson and Pendle Hill, which in the old days was notorious for witchcraft. So there I was in Happy Valley, minus the witches, and very glad to be there. We were in heaven; before us stretched the most glorious sight of golden sandy beaches and a never-ending blue Mediterranean. This piece of heaven belonged to the camp and was private and guarded. Noon until 5 p.m. – off duty; that's all we could think about. We had been told at the meeting that we should spend no longer than an hour on the beach; it was a chargeable offence to get sunburnt.

Our practical joker, Bimbo, who had been posted along with us (unfortunately), insisted she was alright and refused to budge off the beach. She stayed for a further thirty minutes and ended up unable to wear a uniform for four days and forfeited two weeks' wages as a result.

* * *

I soon settled into the routine of army life in Cyprus. I discovered that squash did not quench my thirst and that Coca-Cola did. I learnt not to drive my Land Rover too near the culverts – which were like gullies or ditches – running around the perimeter. I not only drove into one but I also reversed into one; on each occasion having the embarrassment of calling upon the Royal Electrical and Mechanical Engineers (REME) to tow me out.

I was told one evening that a lance corporal and I were to go on escort duties the following day to pick up a brigadier from Nicosia airport, so we spent all evening pressing our uniforms, bulling our shoes and cleaning the Land Rover ready for the journey.

On the way to Nicosia the Land Rover went into a spin, turned round about six times and came to a stop. We looked at each other and burst out laughing. We were covered in sand and all we could see were each others' eyes. We were going to be in serious trouble. I made straight for the Military Police headquarters in Nicosia and we spent the next hour cleaning up. Fortunately the flight was delayed and the brigadier was escorted unaware of the drama that had preceded his arrival.

* * *

After a few months at Episkopi I was posted along with a lance corporal to a WRAC base in Nicosia. The reason for the posting was because the various regiments which patrolled the island and set up roadblocks needed female military police for the purpose of searching Cypriot women.

We went under escort every day, manning roadblocks and searching houses. It never failed to amaze me how many people climbed out of a bus and when we went inside to search we couldn't move for animals and birds. All the women dressed in black and strongly objected to being searched. We didn't like searching them either, but it was a job that had to be done. We were ambushed on more than one occasion, and soldiers were killed or wounded.

I hadn't been in Cyprus long when the patrol I was with set up a roadblock. They stopped a car with four Cypriot men inside and the Corporal in charge told them to get out. He lined them up against the wall with their arms outstretched and feet apart. He then proceeded to kick their feet further and further away from the wall. I didn't think this was right so I said to him, 'Don't do that.'

'You keep out of it,' he replied.

'I won't keep out of it, and what's more I outrank you, so do as you're told or I'll report you.'

'You'll learn,' he said.

Well, I did: when the men got back into their car they drove a short distance and started shooting at us!

I was with the same patrol and we were parked off the road at

38

lunchtime when a shot rang out. The Sergeant who stood with us told us to get under the vehicle. It was a three-tonner so there was plenty of room underneath for me and the Lance Corporal. We didn't know what was going on, and there was a lot of coming and going. We were under there for some time before the Sergeant came back.

'You can come out now,' he said.

'What's happened?' I asked.

'One of the lads has shot himself because he got a "Dear John" letter.'

The Sergeant looked very distressed and so were we when we found out who it was: we had been in his company just the previous evening and all he could talk about was his girl back home. He'd said he was counting the days and would soon be returning to England. He must have received the letter that morning.

On the day he was flown home we attended a service that the regiment arranged as a send-off: this way his friends were able to say goodbye. It was very touching and very sad.

On one occasion we were in convoy travelling up Troodos Mountain. On one side was a sheer drop and I could see army vehicles that had gone over the edge, and on the other side were steep slopes with stones and bushes.

We had been travelling for about an hour when all hell broke loose; we were being attacked by terrorists on the hillside. The convoy came to a stop. I was in a Land Rover with a fellow military policewoman and we were unarmed as we were not allowed to carry arms, but the Lance Corporal who was driving had a Sten gun. We all jumped out into a culvert that ran alongside the road. Our driver was shot, so I grabbed the Sten gun and started shooting back. Suddenly a Cypriot jumped out right in front of us. I think he was startled to see two women because he hesitated briefly. I didn't: I let go with the Sten gun, emptying the machine. Being such a good shot I couldn't miss him, and he just seemed to disappear.

When the shooting stopped we continued on our way in another vehicle as it was thought we would be safer. When we reached camp we were all exhausted and we knew that some of our men had been killed and wounded.

On my way to breakfast the next morning I made my way over to look at the casualty list and right at the bottom it said 'Cpl Waddington [me] shot Cypriot in foot' – so much for being a crack shot!

But men were dying, both British and Cypriot. When I arrived back at base I wrote a poem.

Beyond the reach of Man we stand
On this island of fear where death is ever near
And though it's Christians we profess to be
We shoot on sight whoever we see.
I wonder, my God, is this me?
The people I see are rare and sincere
Yet behind them dwells this fear
I long to show my love of Man
To say a word, to shake a hand
And yet I wonder, my God, who can I trust?
Night is falling, I kneel by my bed
My heart is sick with sorrow
I dare not lift my head
I pray, my God, I pray
Free these people from the fear that holds
That they may live and wonder
Yet never be told
Twas you, my God, whose eyes did rest
And this Island, you did bless.

When the war was over I passed this poem over to a journalist, but I don't know what he did with it. I recall he asked if anything funny had happened to me while serving on the island and I told him about when I was on duty at the prison in Nicosia. The women were being searched when one of them attacked me with a cucumber. He sent the article to the *Nelson Leader*. Relating the story, it said 'Before she knew where she was there were cucumbers flying everywhere.' Typical of a reporter to exaggerate!

Doreen Salmon

* * *

The war that was ongoing at the time was between Greek Cypriots and Turkish Cypriots. I think the Greek Cypriots wanted the island to themselves, but they did not succeed and, about twenty years later, Turkey invaded Cyprus and took over part of the island for the Turkish Cypriots. It remains so today, with a partition running through it which is manned by United Nations troops.

I have since been back to this beautiful island on a number of occasions. The road where I did a spin in the Land Rover is now a motorway and when I drove into Nicosia I couldn't find my way out. Different altogether in comparison, but that's progress.

* * *

The leader of the Greek-Cypriot liberation movement in Cyprus, EOKA, was called George Grivas. He was the head of the movement and he wanted union with Greece. We were forever trying to capture this man. He was sighted on many occasions, but every time we got there he was gone. I think the authorities thought if they captured him the fighting would stop. I don't think that would have been the case because there is always someone waiting in the wings to take over. Apart from which, the leader of the Greek Orthodox Church was in sympathy with the EOKA movement. This leader was eventually removed from the island because of the influence he had over the Cypriot people. This didn't go down too well; I think we made more enemies with the removal of this great spiritual leader.

There was a sense of fear all over the island. I felt sorry for the Cypriots, both Greek and Turkish, living on this beautiful island and not being able to enjoy the pleasures the island afforded them. At the time I didn't appreciate the implications of all that was going on. I was young and enthusiastic, and enjoying life, despite all the tragic events which were taking place around me.

It was during my stay in Nicosia that I received word that Aunty Margaret's husband, Stan, had died. The family wrote asking if I could

41

come home as she was in a bad way and had been asking for me. Fortunately I was at that time engaged to a sergeant in the Special Investigation Branch (SIB) and he was able to get me onto a flight home as I had managed to get two weeks' sick leave.

It was a long and tiring journey. Added to the flight to London was a train journey home, which took about seven hours. By the time I arrived home the funeral was over so I stayed with my aunty.

I hired a car and took her and a friend to Morecambe. When we arrived I couldn't find reverse on the car. Eventually I had to ring the hire firm. I told them I thought there was something wrong with the car because it made a grinding noise on the dual carriageway. He said that the noise was caused by the change of surface on the road. I think he regretted hiring me the car; plus I felt a complete fool!

We went almost daily to Morecambe because I knew Aunty Margaret loved the seaside and it did her the world of good, helping her to recover from the loss of her husband. She had fallen in love with him when he was already a married man and it wasn't until he became free that she was able to marry him. They had been married ten years before he died. It was both romantic and sad. I returned to Cyprus knowing that I had left her in a happier state than the one I had found her in.

* * *

During my tour of duty in Cyprus one event that left an impression on me was being summoned, along with the Lance Corporal I had been working with, to appear before the commanding officer of one of the regiments. We appeared before him dressed in number one uniform, not knowing what to expect. We marched in, saluted and stood to attention. Sitting at his desk, this very high-ranking officer, with a smile on his face, told us that we were doing a wonderful job, that we weren't appreciated like we should be and as a show of gratitude he would like to present us with their royal regimental badge. What an honour! Their most prized possession and they wanted us to be part of it. We thanked him, marched out of the room and promptly burst into tears. By the time we got back to our barracks we had both grown several inches in stature.

A truce was finally reached and we had the freedom of the island. I was posted back to Episkopi and was assigned to a unit that had arrived from the BBC. Another corporal and I toured the island while they filmed us in various locations. We spent a week in their company and when they left they told us they would be showing the film on television but couldn't say when, so I wrote home and told my family to watch out for a documentary on Cyprus. To my knowledge it was never shown. No doubt they will have it stored away somewhere.

Chapter Six

ILEFT CYPRUS WITH A HEAVY heart. My tour of duty had ended and I returned to England, leaving my fiancé behind. He had another year before his tour ended.

I returned to Kingston-upon-Thames with only about three months before my demob date. I was offered sergeant stripes to sign on for another three years. I declined; my intention was to return to civilian life and await my fiancé's return, when we would be married, and we planned to go overseas to Australia.

I returned home and got a job working on the local buses as a clippie. We were called clippies because of the machines we used to clip the tickets with, but officially we were conductors. I fell head over heels in love with my driver, Bill. He lived with another clippie called Lucy. Although Lucy was very nice, I didn't seem to be able to stop myself from falling in love.

I had a beautiful ring on my finger as a constant reminder that I was engaged, but no matter how many times I looked at it and gave myself a good talking-to, I still knew I wanted to be with Bill, so when he told me one morning that Lucy had left him and gone back to Leeds where she came from, I was over the moon. I knew the feeling was mutual and it wasn't long before we started going out together. I wrote to my fiancé and explained that I had fallen in love and said I was sorry to let him down. He wrote back and said he didn't accept it was over and he still wanted to see me on his return to England.

I was smitten by Bill, but I didn't go to live with him. I lived with Aunty Margaret at the time. Then one day he fell down the cellar steps and broke his leg. I went over as often as I could to help him. I arrived one evening with a pie that Aunty Margaret had made for him, and when I walked into the house Lucy was there. She said Bill had rung her and asked her to come. I looked at him and he didn't say a thing. She asked me if I had been going out with him, I said yes and walked out of the house.

The following morning I watched him get off the bus across the road from my house. He explained he had made a mistake, that it was me he wanted and he was sorry. I told him I wasn't interested and sent him away. When I shut the door I watched him hobbling away on his crutches and my heart melted. I ran after him … and I lived to regret it!

It wasn't until I became pregnant that I found out he was already married. I had asked Bill on a number of occasions when we were going to get married, but he always seemed reluctant to set a date. It never entered my head that he might be married because he was living with Lucy when I met him, so when he finally told me I found it hard to believe. I knew his family lived in South Wales, but not that he had a wife there. It was too late for me then to back out of the relationship. My family already looked down on me for living with a man out of wedlock so when I became pregnant I knew I was on my own. I had broken off my engagement for him and all my dreams of happiness were in tatters.

When my ex-fiancé returned to England he came to see me. He couldn't accept that we were finished, and even though he knew I was pregnant, he still wanted to marry me. I refused, and said I was going to stay with the father of my unborn child, even though it meant becoming an unmarried mother, which at that time meant becoming an outcast.

On 9 May 1961 I gave birth to a baby boy. We named him Gary. It was a long and difficult birth and eventually a forceps delivery. We bonded right away. I absolutely adored him and so did his father. Although I was not married I was happy and content. I settled down to family life and to help make ends meet I got a job working evenings at a factory. I was able to socialise, but the friends I made were unmarried mothers like me.

While Bill and I were still working on the buses we had a good income and lived well. It was when I had to give up work to have Gary that we began to argue a lot, mainly about money.

Bill gave up his job on the buses and took the job of verger at our local church. We had a big do there for Gary's christening. The godparents were a couple of Bill's old friends. I found out later that he was having a long-term affair with the godmother!

* * *

When Gary was about six months old we went on holiday to South Wales and stayed with Bill's brother, Trevor, his wife, Rose, and their two children. They made us feel very welcome. In fact, I hardly saw Gary while we were there. Every time we set off for a day or an evening out they insisted we left the baby with them. I met Bill's mother and his sister, who lived with her family in a caravan. I began to feel like part of the family. It was a nice feeling and I look back on it as a happy time, even though I couldn't understand what they were saying half the time, because their Welsh accent was very strong.

Bill's younger brother, who was only sixteen years old, came back with us and stayed for a while. Bill was ten years older than me, and I found out later that he wasn't actually Bill's brother – he was his son!

On 23 April 1964 I gave birth to a baby girl. We named her Shelagh. I didn't bond with my daughter as I did with Gary. I had a long and difficult birth again and at the end of it I had to have a Caesarean. It took me a long time to recover and I was in hospital for three weeks. When I came home I think I must have been suffering from post-natal depression, only in those days it wasn't recognised as such. My daughter was beautiful and she was a good baby. After a time she won my heart, and became as precious to me as my son.

Bill had got divorced by then, but I decided I didn't want to marry him. He worked for a touring firm that ran holidays abroad and I went with him one time to Switzerland. We left baby Shelagh with my brother and his wife – they had a little girl about the same age so it was good of them to offer. We took Gary with us and travelled overland through France. After a long, tiring journey we arrived on a campsite situated on the side of a lake with beautiful scenery. Family tents were already erected and everything we needed was to hand.

We were surrounded by Germans and when I asked the family in the tent next to us if they spoke English, the man retorted, 'Do you speak German? You English always expect us to speak your language, but you don't take the trouble to learn ours!'

So we didn't get off to a good start! But in the end we had some great nights out drinking beer and singing along with the Germans.

The other thing I remember well was having a day out where people skied. Gary wanted to go into a cage car that went up to the top of the mountain, but I've always been afraid of heights and wasn't able to take him. A couple took pity on him, seeing him crying, and took him up with them; he loved it.

The holiday was a joy, but on my return home I was to find out that Bill's job as a coach driver was to be the means of ending our relationship.

He was away for weeks at a time, but it wasn't until I started to receive letters addressed to Mrs Cook that I realised he was having affairs with women who travelled on his coach. The contents of the letters were always along the same lines, but from different women. It didn't dawn on me at first why they were writing to 'Mrs Cook'. I had changed my surname by deed poll to Cook for the sake of the children, so I thought they were writing to me. When the penny dropped I couldn't believe it: he had told them he was living with his mother!

When he came home I showed him the letters.

'I can't help it if I get spinsters on my coach who are looking for a bit of excitement,' he said.

'These are not spinsters. They're young girls saying they've fallen in love with you and what a lovely son I've got!'

When he said, 'We're not married, are we?' I thought, well, that's a good excuse!

It wasn't until one of the women turned up at the house that I learnt more about his carrying on. I was upstairs bathing Gary when I looked out of the back window and saw Bill talking to a woman at the gate leading into the yard. I knew who it was because I had received a letter telling how she was going to be arriving about teatime. I wrapped Gary up in a towel, and went out to the yard to confront them.

'I'm his partner and this is our son Gary,' I said.

Bill tried to push me back into the house.

I shouted, 'He doesn't live with his mother; he lives with me.'

Bill managed to shut the door on me, but I had got my point across. Needless to say, we had a blazing row when he came in.

The woman later wrote to me saying how sorry she was. She said she'd been having a relationship with Bill and thought they were going to get married, but had now broken off the relationship, and asked if she could call round to see me. I didn't reply.

Understandably, I wasn't going to tie myself for life to a man that was unfaithful; he had used up all the love I had for him. I eventually told him to leave and was left on my own with two children. I took in a lodger called Betty and we worked out an arrangement. She had a little boy called Stephen, so I went to work full-time and she stayed at home and looked after the children. This worked very well as Bill was continuing to pay the mortgage. He had put the house in his name, which meant that I had no rights to the property, but I never saw him again.

* * *

I changed my line of work and got a job that came with a company vehicle. I loaded my van up with goods and then set off on an established round that covered Clitheroe, Chatham and Downham: all countryside towns and villages. I collected money for goods that customers had already bought and sold merchandise from my van. I loved my job and was good at selling, so I made a decent wage. Sometimes I picked Aunty Margaret up and took her with me. She brought sandwiches and a flask of coffee with her; I think she enjoyed it as much as I did.

The advantage of having a van meant I was able to go on holiday with it. I set off with my children and went to Blackpool. We looked round for a nice flat or bed and breakfast, and spent many happy hours either on the sands or in Stanley Park.

* * *

I had a number of friends from work and we used to go out at weekends either to Burnley or Blackburn. It was during a night out in Blackburn that I met a man from Australia. He was quite wealthy and took me and the children out on excursions. I was quite fond of him, but he wanted to get married and for us all to go to Australia where he had a ranch. Unfortunately I wasn't in love with him and felt that it was too great a risk. Australia was too far away, so he returned to his homeland without me.

Had my brother still been living out there I think I might have decided differently. It wasn't until I returned home from the approved school that I found out my brother had been sent away shortly after Gwen had got rid of me. When he returned, we attended a youth club at the Church Of Christ, which was a Baptist church. It was there that he met his future wife.

First he had to do his compulsory national service: two years in the Armed Forces. He joined the army and was posted to Egypt. He sent money home each week for saving towards his marriage, but when he returned home, he found out Gwen had spent all his savings, claiming she thought it was for her and father.

Keith married the girl from the youth club and they had three children: all girls. There were a lot of people at that time who emigrated to Australia. It only cost ten pounds, so he took his family out there. They were happy there, but unfortunately the eldest child had asthma and after three years they had to return to England because of the climate. My brother had attended a meeting in Australia conducted by Billy Graham, an American evangelist who was renowned worldwide. When the call went out to be saved he went forward. On his return to England he became a lay preacher.

I'd had no dealings with the church since my childhood. I recall

49

thinking about where we all go when we die. I decided we can't float about in the air because there would be too many bodies. My conclusion was that I would look into it when I was old and passing on would be more relevant.

I had a friend who I thought was a bit odd. She was what the church called a 'backslider'. She was always going on about going back to the church or going back to Jesus. I had no interest in either. I was quite content with my life as it was, so it came as a shock to me when my life was suddenly turned upside down.

I was at home one afternoon, and my friend was sitting on the rug in front of the fire.

'It's no good. I will have to go back to Jesus,' she blurted out.

'If this Jesus you are always on about is so wonderful, how did you get away from him in the first place?' I asked, thinking this was a very clever question.

'Do you want Jesus in your life?'

What a cheek, I thought. She had turned it on me. I couldn't say no because I believed in God, but I couldn't say yes because I knew he didn't want me. If I was an outcast from society there was no way Jesus would want to be part of my life.

'Well, do you or don't you?' she pressed.

'Yes,' I said eventually, taking a leap of faith, knowing full well I would be turned away.

Something happened: the door of my heart opened and someone entered.

'You've got him; I can see it on your face!' exclaimed my friend.

'Well, I've got something, but I've only got your word it's this Jesus.'

'It is, you've got him,' she insisted.

I thought of my Roman Catholic friend Betty, who was living with me at the time.

'Alright, so what do I say to Betty when she comes home? "I know this sounds funny but I've got Jesus in my heart"?'

When I spoke those last words the truth of them was revealed. A cascade of 'living water' flowed through my body, lighting up my very being, creating a spontaneous outpouring of love and joy beyond belief. I couldn't stop smiling, I remember going to the mirror and trying to wipe the grin off my face because my face was aching so much.

I had literally been 'born again'. From that moment on, my life changed. I had entered into a kingdom I knew nothing about. I went to work the following morning and told everyone I had been saved. They all congratulated me and then went on with their work as if I no longer existed. I didn't expect them to understand; I hardly understood myself.

I went to see the elders of the church I had attended in my childhood. I was bursting with enthusiasm, thinking they would be overjoyed. Here were people who understood. Not so. All I witnessed was an embarrassing squirming reaction. In other words, they didn't know what I was talking about. I left utterly confused, but this much I did know: there was something sadly wrong with the church.

I expected them to rejoice, to praise God and jump for joy. Instead of which I got: 'Oh, that's nice' and 'I'm very pleased for you.' The best comment I recall was: 'You're very lucky.' Did this mean it didn't happen to everyone? Well, it certainly didn't happen to everyone like it happened to me and I soon found myself at loggerheads with my fellow Christians. I realised I needed to attend church and accept people as I found them. I reasoned that once I had a better understanding of what had happened to me I would be in a better position to challenge their response.

My friend bought me a Bible and told me to read the Gospel according to Saint John. I read about something that had happened nearly two thousand years ago and realised it was what had happened to me. I was overjoyed, amazed and overcome by the enormity of it. I was learning, and at the same time absorbing, the life of the man who had just entered my heart. I decided that to have a better understanding of God I'd read the Bible from the beginning. By the time I arrived back at the Gospels I understood perfectly who Jesus was, the purpose of his coming and the importance of all he achieved in his short life. I concluded that only a father can explain the nature and make-up of his only son.

I had been doing my best to 'put on the whole armour of God' as I seemed to be getting shot down all the time. When a dean who was the head of a university in Manchester arrived at the church we were told he would be staying for a week, so I took the opportunity to ask him to explain how to put the armour on. He told me we would have to study the scriptures as it was not easily explained. So I arranged for him to visit me at home one evening. I also arranged for my friend to come along.

I recall the evening being long and drawn-out. He quoted chapter and verse. If his intention was to baffle us, he succeeded. He didn't baffle us entirely, though, because we realised by the end of the evening that he didn't know how to put on the armour.

I was left with this thought: If a man of letters doesn't understand the fundamental teachings of the written word, then what chance do we have?

These leaders of the church were a great disappointment to me, but I was not discouraged. I received instructions from a different source.

I was fortunate in so much as I found a kindred spirit in a lay preacher called Fred, who was an excellent preacher of the Gospel. He took me with him to the various churches he preached at so I could testify to the event that had taken place, and I stood in the pulpit and gave it my all. After the meetings people hung around in small groups, talking about everyday things, and no reference was made about what I had said, or for that matter, what Fred had said.

Chapter Seven

I HAD BEEN LIVING IN BURNLEY for a number of years when I decided to move back to my hometown of Nelson. I didn't have a house to live in so the children and I stayed with my friend and her husband until we found somewhere of our own.

Shelagh had been having recurring nightmares about a dog coming into her room and attacking her. She said she called out for me, but I never went to her. We had been awaiting an appointment to see a psychologist when we were still living in Burnley. She was rapidly losing weight, and I was becoming very anxious because the waiting list was so long. She was only seven years old and I knew it could have a lasting effect on her if something wasn't done.

One evening we stayed over at a friend's house to attend a meeting at church. I was worried about leaving Shelagh. I said to my friend, 'I don't like leaving her. What if she has another nightmare and I am not here?'

'When you put her to bed I will go in and pray for her,' she said.

I didn't go in with her, but when she came out she told me that she had asked the Lord to take the dog away. I left believing he would answer my friend's prayer.

When I returned, Shelagh was fast asleep and no one had heard her cry out, which was what she usually did. The following morning I asked her if the dog had been.

'No,' she said, 'Jesus took it away.'

The dog never returned. Shelagh put on weight and was a much happier child.

One of a Kind

* * *

One evening I had been to a Pentecostal church, which believed in 'Baptism in the Holy Spirit', whereas the church I normally attended was a Baptist church that believed in 'Baptism in Water'.

I had seen the children off to bed and had settled down with my Bible, intent on finding out where the truth lay. I was sitting comfortably with my feet up on the mantelpiece when I heard a rustling noise coming from round the back of the settee behind me. I got up off my chair and went to look, but there was nothing there. I sat back down, put my feet up again and had just started to read again when I heard the rustling sound again, only this time it seemed to be getting louder. I thought it was Gary, out of bed and messing about, but then I heard Gary upstairs, so I settled back down.

It wasn't long before I heard the rustling again. Being satisfied in my mind that it wasn't the children, I sat still and listened. It sounded like leaves blowing in the wind. Gradually it grew in momentum, gathered into a whirlwind that came round the end of the settee and as it hovered above my head it dropped a scripture, and then disappeared.

I knew this was a message from God, but didn't know who had delivered it. I didn't move, I just sat there and savoured the moment. After a while I opened my Bible to the scripture that the whirlwind had dropped over my head (*1 Corinthians 3: 2*). It read: 'I have fed you with milk, and not with meat: for hitherto ye were not able to bear it, neither yet now are ye able.' My reaction was one of amazement. I had received instructions from this wonderful kingdom I had just been born into and, the shame of it; I had my feet up on the mantelpiece!

The following week we had a Bible study at my friend's house. It was a lovely sunny evening and the children were playing out on the back street. I had to leave the meeting because a fight broke out that involved my two, so I brought them in and put them to bed as I had already arranged for us to stay the night.

As a result I missed the Bible study and I said to the Lord, 'How do you expect me to learn when my children are playing up all the time?' Into my head popped *Romans 8: 18*. I was fairly new to the scriptures, but I knew this one: 'All things work together for good to them that love God'. I had none of it. I thought this was a cop-out; something to quote when not giving a straight answer.

'No,' I said. 'I'm not having it: it's not good enough.'

Some may think this was disrespectful, but I had been deprived of my Bible study that I had been looking forward to all week. So each time *Romans 8: 18* came into my mind I repeated, 'No. I'm not having it.'

Eventually I went into the front room so I could be on my own. I sat down and said, 'Alright, Lord, I will read the scripture, but I know what it's going to say.'

I opened my Bible and read *Romans 8: 18* and this is what it said: 'For I reckon that the sufferings of this present time are not worthy to be compared with the Glory that shall be revealed in us.'

Not only had I got the wrong scripture (*Romans 8: 28*), but I had been far too clever for my own good. I was eternally grateful for this wonderful passage that has been a comfort to me throughout the trials which were to beset me.

* * *

I had a zeal for God that knew no boundaries; whether at work, on the street or in church, I talked about Jesus. People at work or in the street didn't want to know, which I could accept. The church was a different matter, however. I couldn't accept how things were and I was slowly being drawn into the way of life of a churchgoer. I didn't want to be a hypocrite; I considered the church in general to be fast asleep, and because I was not willing to compromise I decided eventually to leave the church and to keep my own counsel.

While I was staying with my friend, my brother put us in touch with a man called Douglas, an inmate at Kirkham Open Prison. We visited him and did our best to help him, but he sent letters saying he had fallen in love with me. I didn't have any romantic feelings towards him. When he was discharged from prison he stayed with us for a weekend. We knew his problem was alcohol, but he assured us that he was never going to drink again … After he left we found a large glass dish in a drawer, full of urine! So much for not drinking. I was just thankful I had been able to keep him at arm's length and we parted friends – of a sort.

I had learnt a valuable lesson. Although I wanted to help people, I decided that different people live in different worlds and there are many pitfalls that do-gooders are not aware of. I decided I was as well tending to my own business instead of trying to put other people's lives to rights.

* * *

I was no longer able to travel to Burnley to work so I got a job working from home sewing ties. It didn't pay much, but it meant that I could be at home to look after my children. I started having problems with Gary. He had started at a new school that was situated just two streets away from where we lived. When he came home at teatime I asked him if he'd had a nice day.

'These boys keep picking on me. They wanted to fight and I wouldn't,' he told me one day.

'Is that why you've got a bruise on your face?' I asked.

This became a regular conversation. I decided to wait for him outside school as most of the bullying took place at hometime. I even got to speak to some of the lads.

'Why do you keep hitting Gary?' I asked.

''Cos he's a big softy; he won't fight,' one of them replied.

'What's wrong with that? He's been brought up not to fight.'

All they did was shrug their shoulders and walk away.

It didn't change anything and I began to think it was my fault for telling him it was wrong to fight. He ran away from home, which just added to the problem. I knew he was intelligent, but he was something of a 'Walter Mitty', living in a fantasy world. He left me a note one day that said 'I am going to seek my fortune. If I am not back by 9 May, call the police'. This was his birthday. Each time he ran away I had to call the police because he was only twelve years old.

Eventually the police decided to take him to court. They told me, 'He can't keep running away like this. He is going to come to some harm if he carries on.'

The court ruled that he was out of parental control and ordered that he should be sent to a care home in Blackburn. I was heartbroken. I was worried because he didn't get on with other boys and thought he might be bullied. I didn't think he'd done anything wrong, so he didn't deserve it. I was allowed to see him before they took him away. I tried to assure him he would be alright, while all the time my heart was crying out, wanting to protect him. He didn't cry. He just said, 'I'll be alright, Mum.' I went home and shed enough tears for both of us.

Blackburn was about fifteen miles away and he kept running away from the school. On one occasion he followed the railway tracks back to Nelson, so they moved him further afield to a place in Yorkshire, which made it more difficult for visiting. He sent me a pass to visit every month and I did my best to visit as often as I could. I knew he was unhappy there and he got picked on. After visiting, I returned home and cried myself to sleep. The saying goes: 'Have a good cry; it will make you feel better', but it never did.

On one visit Shelagh and I were sitting at a table, waiting for Gary to arrive. When he walked towards us I could see that he didn't look at all well. I asked him what was wrong.

'Nothing. I'm alright,' he said.

But when he sat down I noticed that he had cuts on both wrists. I asked him what he had done, but he wouldn't tell me, so I went and asked to speak to someone in authority.

'Gary had problems with some of the boys, so we put him in a room with another boy who had similar problems. While Gary was asleep the boy slashed Gary's wrists,' I was told.

'I can't believe this,' I said.

'If you want to take it further, you can do.'

I told Gary he should put in a complaint, but he said he didn't want any more trouble, so we had to leave it at that.

When Gary came home he was unable to settle. After a short time he left home and went to Rhyl where he found lodgings and a job. Eventually he wrote to say not to worry about him as he would be alright. I didn't hear from him again until I got a visiting order for him in prison. He had been arrested for burglary.

I went with Shelagh to visit him. We were not allowed to leave any of the things we had brought for him and were only allowed to see him briefly, but just seeing him was enough. It meant I could hold him and tell him how much I loved him. Had I known what was to happen to him in the future, it is as well that we don't know what lies ahead.

* * *

It was when I was living in Nelson that I met my future husband. I had called round to see Aunty Margaret who worked at a garage. She made a brew and asked me to take a cup of tea to a man who was working round the back of the garage. He was digging a pit for the cars to go over.

When I called in later on in the week he was still there. I found out his name was Edwin Salmon and he was a plasterer by trade. I kept calling round, hoping I would see him. I think he was down that pit about three weeks. I was attracted to him and I think the feeling was mutual. When my aunty told me he was married I decided it was going nowhere and I stopped calling round.

One Friday evening he turned up at my house with a tray of eggs that my aunty had asked him to deliver. Well, I couldn't leave him on the doorstep so I invited him in. He told me that he and his wife were not getting on together, but that he didn't want to leave because he had four children. I told him that it wouldn't be right for us to see each other while he was married, but he continued to come each Friday with a tray of eggs.

Eventually Eddie found out his wife had been having an affair and they separated. They came to an arrangement that Eddie would have two of the children living with him and pay maintenance towards the other two. His wife left the marital home and went to live with her lover.

He lived in Earby, about ten miles away. He worked seven days a week and it took me a while to persuade him to take Sundays off. We took the children out into the countryside or sometimes to Morecambe for the day. Eddie loved fishing and we all sat by the river and had a picnic. I eventually talked him into taking the whole weekend off and we bought some camping equipment and travelled all over, pitching the tent wherever we found a nice idyllic spot with a river close by. We had what we called wakes holidays, which meant they were taken at the same time each year, in July. We spent one week in Scotland, then travelled down the motorway and spent the second week in Morecambe.

We finally decided that we didn't want to live apart any longer, and I left Nelson to live with Eddie in Earby. This made the most sense because Eddie's house had three bedrooms and mine only had two. We had already bonded as a family and I thought everything would work out alright. He asked his wife for a divorce and although she said no, we thought she was just being spiteful and would come round in time.

I got a job and settled down to family life in Earby. It wasn't easy. When children are thrown together from different marriages there are all sorts of problems. I blamed his children and he blamed mine. They got into trouble and fought all the time. But there were good times as well. We still camped at weekends and went on holiday every year.

Eventually we moved from Earby to Colne: a small town situated next to my hometown of Nelson and also the place where Eddie worked.

All the houses Eddie and I had lived in until then had been corporation houses. I bought new curtains, towels and a school uniform for Shelagh. On the day we moved in I took all our new purchases, including Shelagh's school shirts and PE kit, to the launderette opposite our street and set off with Shelagh to town to do the shopping. I told her they'd all be done by the time we got back. I had already washed them, but we didn't have a dryer, so I reckoned they would take about an hour.

When we got back to the launderette, the dryer was empty: someone had stolen all our new things. I took an instant dislike to Colne.

I managed to find employment at the cotton mill nearby. It was shift work and I was employed to put the shuttles onto a machine, wait for them to fill up and take them off. It was so boring I thought my brain would seize up, but the pay was good.

I stuck at it for as long as I could. Then one day I went home for my half-hour break and never went back. I should have handed in my notice, but I had let it go on too long: I just came to a stop.

Eddie's eldest son had been pestering him, wanting to go into the army. Eddie did his best to discourage him; having been in the army himself, he didn't think it would be suitable for him. He let him go eventually and said: 'If you're determined to join up then you will have to stick it out.'

It wasn't long before he discharged himself. His father was right; he wasn't cut out for army life. He took up plastering instead and eventually became a successful businessman.

* * *

We hadn't been living in Colne long when I woke up one morning feeling poorly, so I went to the doctor's surgery. The doctor examined me and said, 'You're having a miscarriage. Is there anyone at home?'

'No,' I said, 'but I can ring my partner at work. He will come home.'

'Right, go straight home. I'm going to ring for an ambulance.'

I went home and rang Eddie, who arrived at the same time as the ambulance. He couldn't believe it. Neither could I: we didn't even know I was pregnant.

I lost the baby: it was a girl. I was very upset. Eddie visited in the evening, and all I wanted was to go home.

'Bring my clothes when you come tomorrow night,' I told him.

He did this a few evenings running; then he went to see the

60

matron, who then came to see me.

'Don't keep asking for your clothes,' she told me. 'You will go home when we decide you are well enough, and not before.'

Poor Eddie. Every night he thought I was coming home. We had a good laugh about it later on, though.

When we looked back on the loss of our child, we came to the conclusion that had she lived our lives might have been different. A baby born into the family would have been the centre of attention and the binding of two families. It may have been wishful thinking on our part, but we would have been happy to have a baby of our own out of the love we had for each other.

We eventually decided to live separately in order to give ourselves a chance because it wasn't working with the children, so we each rented a house in Colne just one street away from each other, and things started to improve. We were a lot happier and, best of all, Eddie's wife had agreed to give him a divorce.

* * *

It was when I was living on my own with Shelagh that I began to have problems. She skipped school and became rebellious, staying out late. I felt like it was a constant battle. I don't know if it was because of living with Eddie's children, who she didn't get along with, but once we were living on our own I had thought things would improve.

Once she went missing for two nights. I was frantic with worry, and finally found out that she had been staying with a young man. I became afraid for her safety and the path she was setting herself to go on, so I arranged for her to go to a private school run by nuns.

I felt a complete failure and blamed myself. I had lost both my son and my daughter. To this day I chastise myself because I know in some part it was my fault. My children would disagree with me, but I know the proportion of blame that is mine.

* * *

After being together for about three years, Eddie and I finally got married. It was a lovely wedding and Shelagh was allowed home to attend. Keith, who had by then moved to Devon and remarried, came home to give me away. It was a very happy occasion, with all my relatives and friends there. My father, unfortunately, was not well enough to attend, and Gwen was not invited.

A friend of my husband's, who owned a garage, lent us a car for two weeks as a wedding present, and we went to stay with Keith and his wife in Devon for our honeymoon. It was different altogether from being up north. Life was lived at a slower pace and we didn't witness the poverty that was so apparent up north. We thoroughly enjoyed our two-week stay, but we had to travel back on the inside lane of the motorway all the way home because we had problems with the car.

We arrived home to find Eddie's eldest son in hospital. He had been out in the countryside on his motorbike, had gone round a bend and straight into a cow. He had a broken arm and a broken leg. He and his brother had decided not to let us know as they didn't want to spoil our honeymoon. When he came home he was in plaster for weeks and unable to work. I think he wanted to sue the farmer who owned the cow, but I don't recall him succeeding.

On our return we were offered a three-bedroom council house in Nelson. I was very pleased to return to Nelson. The house had a small garden at the front and a large garden at the back; it was the nicest house I had ever lived in. When it became law that council tenants could buy their houses, we applied to buy ours and eventually we owned it.

* * *

I went to work at a home for the elderly. I really enjoyed my job. I felt that I was doing something meaningful and found that I had an easy rapport with the elderly. I worked there for about two years before I went on a course and qualified with sufficient results to enable me to become a relief deputy. This meant that if the head of a home was off sick or on leave I was called in to run the home. Therefore I travelled all

Doreen Salmon

over the Pendle area to different homes – some large and some small – but they all presented a challenge. I was only about one year into my new role when I slipped at work and injured my shoulders. I was off work for a few weeks, but when I returned I found I was unable to continue due to the lifting aspect of the job. I was very disappointed; I had worked hard to get to this stage and had dreamed of becoming a permanent head of my own home for the elderly one day.

It was at this time that Shelagh returned home. I was glad to have her back, but she soon found work and moved into a bedsit in Colne. I was apprehensive about her being on her own, but she wanted her independence, as all young people do.

She fell in love with a local boy, but it didn't work out. On the rebound she married a man because she got pregnant and didn't want the child to be born out of wedlock. Eddie and I agreed she should get married for the sake of the child. She gave birth to a little boy called Earl. The marriage got into trouble, though, and her husband turned violent. She moved away to Blackburn to get away from him. Under the pretext of wanting to see his son he tried to track her down, so she reverted back to her maiden name and changed her son's name to Aaron.

We had a touring caravan and at one stage had to resort to taking Shelagh and Aaron away for a while to give her a break from her husband, who was ringing all the time and threatening her. He even turned up outside the house, revving his car engine and threatening to drive into the house.

Shelagh eventually took him to court where he was ordered to pay just five pence a week in maintenance because he wasn't working. The court ruled that he could see Aaron under supervision for two hours every other Saturday. He never once showed up. It seemed to us that this proved he had just wanted to get to Shelagh.

He eventually took up with someone else and so things slowly went back to normal. It was a very traumatic and stressful time for all of us.

* * *

Aunty Margaret was taken ill while I was working in the homes. I remember going to her house from work and sleeping there overnight. It was very tiring, but I felt I owed her that much. She was the only one who showed any care towards me and Keith when we were young.

One evening when I was there she had a stroke and was admitted to hospital. I phoned Keith and told him what had happened. He came up from Devon right away. His wife had been diagnosed with leukaemia and was not well, so it was a difficult time for him. We went to visit Aunty Margaret each afternoon and evening. Over a period of seven days she slowly started to improve, so on the seventh day Keith returned home to Devon. I recall telling him to wait – I had seen this happen with the elderly; sometimes they seem to recover and then suddenly die. He was anxious to return to his wife, though, and rightly so.

He had just walked into his house when I called to tell him she had died that afternoon.

It was a very emotional time. She had been there all my life and we had shared so many good and bad times together. It was the end of an era: my father had passed away the year before.

* * *

We didn't know our father had been taken into hospital until someone inadvertently mentioned it. Gwen didn't want me or Keith to know. He had been ill for a long time with asthma and bronchitis – I remember he had a bottle of gas and air at his bedside for a number of years. He was always a heavy smoker – either Capstan Full Strength, if he could afford it, or Woodbines if he hadn't much money. I think that, combined with going out in all weathers collecting for Relay, brought about his downfall. As soon as I heard I went to see him. Gwen didn't like me being there and tried to make out that he wasn't all that bad. I could tell he was bad, though; he could hardly speak and was trying to catch his breath all the time. While he was in hospital, she went off to Israel on a seven-day biblical tour. She was a regular churchgoer; she even gave lectures at church meetings. She was a wicked woman, but she didn't want anyone to know.

When my father came out of hospital, it was in a coffin. I had been able to spend some time with him in hospital and had pretended everything was alright because I didn't want to upset him, and I wanted our final times together to be peaceful. I knew in his own way that he loved me, but he was a weak man who was unable to stand up to his wife. I held no ill feelings towards him. If I felt anything, it was a combination of love and sorrow for what might have been.

When it came to the funeral, Keith and his wife attended, which was a comfort. I couldn't stop crying in the church or after. When we left the crematorium, a young woman about my age got into the car with us.

'Who are you?' I asked.

'I'm Eileen, Aunt Gwen's niece.'

I wondered what she was doing there, as she had nothing to do with my father. I didn't realise it at the time, but it seemed Gwen was giving us a statement; letting us know that her interests now lay with her side of the family.

We knew my father had left a will leaving everything to her, and we also knew he didn't have a choice. We think that was why she didn't want us to see him before he died, in case we got him to change his will. We had never mentioned anything about it and I suppose it was beyond her comprehension that we just wanted to be with him, knowing that he wouldn't be with us much longer.

Shortly after my father died I made an attempt to be friendly with Gwen. I thought at some stage she would acknowledge that she was wrong to treat us the way she had. As it turned out it was a waste of time. Keith said she would never admit anything because to her mind she hadn't done anything wrong.

* * *

When Gwen died she left everything to her niece: our home and everything in it. I was very upset that Eileen was to inherit our home, which belonged to us as a family before Gwen came on the scene.

Keith went to see her when she was in hospital and told her she was wicked and was going to hell. He later received a warning letter from her solicitor to stay away.

After she died I received a letter from her solicitor saying that she had left me two hundred pounds. I told him to give it to charity. It was less money for her niece to get her hands on. I never did like her: to my mind she was a chip off the old block.

* * *

One evening I was rushed into hospital with terrible pains in my chest. The doctor told Eddie to take me in the car and that he would radio ahead to let them know we were on our way. When I reached hospital I was wheeled into a cubicle and they took my temperature. I heard the nurse say, 'Either there is something wrong with this thermometer or she shouldn't be here.'

I went into shock. I was very ill; apparently there was something wrong with my gullet and gall bladder. I was in Burnley General Hospital (where my son was to spend so much time). The treatment I received was no better than animals are treated. After ten days of being seriously ill, I was taken for a stomach examination. This consisted of pushing a pipe – which resembled a hosepipe – down my throat. When I choked on it the consultant asked me if I wanted to get better, insinuating that I was being soft as this was normal procedure.

They tried again, without success, so then gave me some white liquid to swallow – the idea being it would outline my stomach when I went for an X-ray the following day. This proved to be useless as it didn't show anything.

I was given a bowl of water to wash my hands and face, then after a few days my daughter asked the ward sister if she could give me a bed bath. I complained about not getting painkillers when they were due, only to be told all the staff were busy. When I threatened to report them, the sister said, 'Good. I hope you do. Maybe then they will realise how short of staff we are.'

The extraordinary event that took place during my stay in

hospital happened sometime during the night. At first all I heard were voices: 'You're bad, you're bad. Unclean, unclean.' I thought at first I was dreaming. I lifted the sheet and looked down my left side. There between my hip and ribs sat three elf-like figures chanting, 'You're bad, you're bad.' They were eating something in their tiny hands and it dawned on me that they were eating the flesh from my side! I knew then what they were; evil emanated from them. I started screaming and they looked up at me with what I can only describe as exultation in their eyes. I was being attacked by demons! My heart started racing. I was so afraid I thought I was going to choke on an all-consuming fear.

'You can't do this. I belong to Jesus,' I said.

They looked up and continued to eat away; it made no difference. By this time there was a big hole in my side. I kept screaming for Jesus to help me, but nothing happened. All the while I looked at these three evil beings eating away at me, chanting, 'You're bad, you're bad. We're going to eat you all up.'

I believed them. I became conscious of all the badness in me and I knew if I didn't stop them I was going to die. It was then I remembered a scripture from my Bible: 'The blood of Jesus Christ cleanses us from all unrighteousness.' I quoted this to the demons. They looked up as if acknowledging the words, then continued to eat me. Over and over I repeated the words; they were the only lifeline I had, but it had no effect. An overwhelming feeling of despair engulfed me, and it was at this point that the power of God took over.

'The blood of Jesus Christ cleanses us of all unrighteousness,' I repeated, and God took over the last two words: 'all unrighteousness', over and over, stronger and stronger until the words literally spewed out of my mouth.

The demons looked up and, realising who they were dealing with, disappeared. I lay back on my pillow and felt relief flow through my body. 'There but for the grace of God,' I thought.

The next morning I expected people on the ward to ask me why I had screamed and shouted during the night. But everyone went about as normal. And when I lifted the sheet up, fully expecting to see a big hole in my side, there was no hole. Everything was as if it hadn't happened.

I learnt two things from this experience. First of all, I always thought that demons were fantasy, make believe. Not so. I believe they are real, they exist, they are evil, and they are the devil's own advocates. Secondly, scripture can be quoted until you are blue in the face, but it isn't until the power of God works with the word that miracles happen.

* * *

I was in hospital for about three weeks, after which I was allowed home for a weekend on the understanding that I returned as an in-patient so they could run some further tests. I finally had my gall bladder removed, by which time I had lost three stone in weight. I still take medicine for my gullet.

Chapter Eight

WE NO LONGER HAD CHILDREN at home, so Eddie and I decided to put a deposit down on a two-bedroom terraced house in Wenning Street on the outskirts of Nelson, taking a small mortgage over five years. There wasn't a proper road as such; it was what was called unadopted, and because of the surface condition not many cars came along at first, so it was very quiet. A proper road was eventually put in and then it became quite busy with vans making deliveries to a working men's club at the top of the street. I think everyone got upset because we had lost that solitude.

Opposite the house there were garages and beyond that allotments. We managed to get a lease for a garage and Eddie acquired an allotment.

We got a dog called Bonnie from some friends we knew on the Isle of Skye. We had gone to visit and they had three dogs. They all bedded down in a shed at the back of the house, but they were allowed in during the day. When they all bounded in on the first day we were there, a lovely white Skye terrier jumped straight into my lap. I took to her so much that I asked our friends if we could take her back home with us. Thankfully they said yes.

On the first day back home we lost her! Eddie had taken her for a walk on the nearby golf course and a cow popped its head over the wall, making Bonnie bolt. Eddie came back home intending to get the car to go looking for her, but she had found her own way back and was sitting waiting for him. I don't know how she managed that, but we were both happy not to have lost her. She was very timid and vulnerable with other dogs so we decided to get a border collie for her protection; we called him Clyde. When Bonnie died we buried her on the allotment where she loved to spend time with my husband and me.

All of the houses on Wenning Street became eligible for a government grant and were to be modified to a high standard. When we heard about this we saw the potential to make some money. The value of the houses, prior to modernisation, was in the region of seven thousand pounds each and there were two houses for sale on our street. We couldn't afford to buy one, but we knew that if we could then we could make a substantial amount of money. I wrote to Keith and asked him if he wanted to go halves with the purchase. He didn't hesitate. He saw the potential of their value once the work was completed.

We bought one of the houses and eventually sold it for fifteen thousand pounds to Eddie's second-eldest son, Raymond. He had been living in rented accommodation and had decided to branch out and buy a house. He worked making mattresses so he had a good income. Raymond loved fishing and riding his motorbike. Unfortunately a few years ago he had just turned forty and, having sold his bike, decided to take it for one last run before parting with it. He crashed the bike on the road to Gisburn, a road notorious for bikers with all the twists and turns. Other bikers who were on the road at the time said they saw Raymond overtake a car on the Settle bypass. He wasn't speeding so we think he must have lost control by skidding. He landed on the other side of a wall and died on impact.

Eddie's eldest son, Mark, erected a stone plaque at the spot where Raymond died, but the corporation made him take it down, so he ended up putting it in a river where Raymond used to go fishing. His ashes were also sprinkled there. Eddie goes there every year on the anniversary of his death with flowers, and also wants his own ashes sprinkled there when the time comes.

* * *

We spent many years living on Wenning Street. We were in a position at that time to have frequent holidays abroad. We once went abroad on holiday to Portugal where we met a couple from Halifax. They went golfing every day and Eddie, who had never been golfing before in his life, went with them and took to it like a duck to water. When we got back home I hardly ever saw him and had to put my foot down; I was fast becoming a golfer's widow!

* * *

Shelagh worked in Accrington for a man who owned several petrol stations. He asked her to manage two of his petrol stations in Manchester, to which she agreed. I asked her if she thought I could manage to run the one in Accrington, so she arranged for me to have an interview and I got the job. I was in my element: I was once again in charge of something and being paid came as a bonus. It wasn't long before I was managing two stations in Manchester as well, although Shelagh's stations were bigger and further away. We both enjoyed our work, even though it meant travelling a long distance each day. We were well paid, but we had to earn our money. We were not only responsible for the running of the stations, taking tankers and ordering stock, but we were also responsible for all the paperwork the job entailed. We took everything in our stride and ran the four stations efficiently. All this was about to change quite suddenly.

* * *

Shelagh had met a man with whos she fell in love. They struck up a relationship, settled down and she gave birth to three more boys. He was a lovely young man and we all thought the world of him. Problems started when he couldn't find work. He became restless and started smoking cannabis. I think he became depressed. I know Shelagh did all she could to make him happy, but he changed and, although she loved him, she had to consider the children, and eventually he moved out and rented a house in Burnley. Although they were no longer living together, they tried to work things out. He had been living in the rented house for a few months when he was found dead. He had accidently overdosed on drugs. It was a terrible tragedy.

Four days after his death, the police knocked on her door, asking if she was related to Gary Cook. She informed them that he was her brother. Gary was studying at Plymouth University and was living in a rented flat. Gary had been found in his flat in Plymouth with severe head injuries and they said that close relatives should make their way there straightaway.

Shelagh rushed round to my house.

'We have to go down there straightaway, Mum.'

'No,' I said. 'I'm not having it.' I just could not accept what I was being told.

She went to Plymouth with two of her friends and with an added worry: my reaction to the news.

That evening I was busy doing the month-end books for work.

'Don't you think you should ring your Keith?' Eddie said eventually.

It was while I was telling Keith what had happened that the reality dawned on me and I started crying. I told him to expect me down there the following day.

Eddie wasn't able to travel with me, so I collected Aaron and took him with me for company. It was a long and tiring journey. We didn't arrive at Keith's until early evening and I was too exhausted to go to the hospital, which was an hour and a half's journey from Keith's. I decided to rest up and prepare myself for going the next day.

When my daughter arrived at Keith's it was nearly midnight. She looked awful; she had travelled through the night and been at the hospital all day.

'You will have to prepare yourself, Mum,' she warned me.

The police were waiting to see if it was going to be a case of manslaughter or murder as it was touch and go for a while, and we were told on numerous occasions to prepare ourselves for the worst.

The next morning I set off with Shelagh and Aaron to the hospital in Plymouth. I didn't know what to expect; I only knew I was dreading seeing my son. We went straight to the ward. The first person we encountered was a policeman who wanted to speak to me.

'No,' I said, pushing past him. I had to see Gary.

I approached the bed where my son lay. His head was very heavily bandaged, and he had a deep scar on the side of his face (I later discovered this had been made with a claw hammer).

'Oh, Gary,' I said, stroking his arm. I remember I kept saying the same thing over and over again. He couldn't hear me, though; he was in a coma. I looked up and saw Aaron had tears streaming down his face.

The consultant told us Gary was in a critical condition and he was in a dreadful state when they had first brought him in due to the fact that he had lain in his flat for five days undetected. An infection had set in where his brain had been damaged as a result of being hit with a claw hammer, his body was burnt with the acid from his urine, and he had a broken bone in his throat where he had been strangled. They'd had to wire up his jaw and his toes were likely to fall off due to frostbite. The consultant wouldn't know the extent of the brain damage until Gary recovered: the next few days were crucial.

I don't know at what point I started crying, but once I started I couldn't stop. I remember Shelagh leading me into the corridor where I leant against a wall for support.

I stayed at his bedside all day, trying to come to terms with what had happened. I was faced with a situation from which there was no escape. My son had been brutally attacked and I had to deal with the aftermath. I wasn't capable of dealing with a conversation, let alone the suffering that involved feelings to the depth of which I found myself plunging. Grief and despair overcame me. It was as if my life had been taken over by the event in which I had become embroiled, so much so that I had to be led about and spoken to softly in case someone upset me. How ridiculous to be found in a situation where I was upset beyond measure and yet was aware that people are trying not to upset me.

We left the hospital late that evening and returned to Keith's house where there was only one topic of conversation. We decided that the next day we would speak to the police and find out what had actually happened.

The following day we all travelled to Derriford Hospital. There was no change in Gary's condition.

'He doesn't deserve this,' said Keith.

No one deserves this, I thought. How anyone can do this kind of thing is beyond me. I became upset again, so when the police approached us I was unable to talk to them. Shelagh was the first to find out what had happened.

Gary's landlady hadn't seen him about and when the rent was due she let herself into his flat. She had found him on the floor barely alive. She phoned the police and ambulance. The detective told Shelagh they were looking for two men in their early twenties who had been seen talking to Gary in a pub the last time he had been seen. They were also looking for the claw hammer used in the attack. They suspected robbery to be the motive as Gary had just received his university grant and no money was found in his flat. The police also told her that they had notified all known close relatives as this was normal procedure if there was any doubt that the injured party would recover.

I received a phone call from his Uncle Trevor, Bill's brother. He told me Gary had contacted him, trying to trace his father. Trevor had told Gary that Bill had moved to France and died of cancer some years ago.

Gary's ex-wife travelled down from Warrington when she heard. I had hoped that he would settle down, especially when his wife gave birth to twins, Benjamin and Emma, but they weren't married long before he left. She didn't stay long, though; I think she travelled home the following day.

When we arrived back at Keith's, the news about Gary was on the local television station. It showed the flat and the police searching the River Hoe in Plymouth for the claw hammer. I couldn't associate the pictures with my son. I often saw such images of the police looking for a murder weapon or some sort of evidence to a crime, but to identify these goings on with a member of my own family was incomprehensible. I looked at the images and followed the story, but couldn't think of Gary in this context. The news was ongoing over the next few weeks as the story unfolded.

It became a wearisome journey travelling back and forth to Plymouth, sitting by Gary's bedside every day, willing him to wake up.

There being no change in his condition, we frequented the hospital's cafeteria, taking it in turns to break up the vigilance.

The news media asked for a photograph of Gary. It wasn't long before his photo was also shown on the local television station. The interest in Gary seemed to increase. There were reporters outside the hospital, but the police wouldn't let them in; even Gary's friends from university were denied access. We had a phone call from our local paper, the *Nelson Leader*, and the *Burnley Express* as Gary was born in Burnley. They showed the river where they looked for the claw hammer and then the flat where my son had been living.

The police eventually arrested two men for the atrocious attack as a result of a conversation they'd had with someone in a café the morning after the attack. This person had been having a full English breakfast and boasted that they had killed someone. Thankfully this was not the case.

The two men had met up with Gary while having a drink in a pub. They were not friends of his, but were known to him through other friends. They had found out that he had just received his university grant of two thousand pounds. They returned with Gary to his flat, plied him with drink and waited until he fell asleep before attacking him with the claw hammer. Believing they had killed him, they decided to make sure by strangling him with his belt. They then took his money and left.

By the time they were caught the money had been spent. For the sake of two thousand pounds they were willing to commit murder. I couldn't see any reasoning to it.

To this day Gary has the mark of a claw hammer on the side of his face and in his head, there is a bone that is still broken in his throat from when they tried to strangle him, and his jaw is permanently wired from when they broke it. So why all the violence? I believe it can only mean that these two men were violent by nature and must have found pleasure in attacking Gary. It also told me that they were cowards; why else would they wait until he fell asleep? To my mind and that of all my family and friends, these men were evil. They were eventually charged with attempted murder and remanded in custody to await trial.

I have not led a sheltered life and I knew about suffering of a kind, but nothing had prepared me for this. I didn't cope well with all that was going on and decided it would be best for me to return home. Neither I nor Shelagh had any money coming in. I was grateful to Keith and his wife for providing us with a home where we felt able to rest and recuperate. Without them we would have had to stay in a hotel, which would have meant expenses greater than those which we had already incurred and it would have added to the stress which we had to cope with. I needed to go home and get back to work, not only for the money, but for my own peace of mind.

Shelagh said, 'If you go now, Mum, I bet Gary will come round.'

Having waited all that time for him to recover, I didn't believe it. She was right, though; he recovered consciousness the next day. She said that when he came to he was crying a lot. The consultant assessed his injuries and said he was paralysed down his right side and he was not able to walk; not only because of the paralysis, but because his feet were twisted. I was thankful I didn't have to witness his recovery. I think it would have been more than I was able to stand.

At least we could go forward. Shelagh requested he be transferred to Burnley General Hospital and arrangements were made for an ambulance to take him home. Shelagh said she wasn't going home without him, and she followed the ambulance all the way home. She was a blessing to her brother and a blessing to me. I would never have got through the ordeal without her. As for Derriford Hospital and the detective in charge of the case, I have nothing but praise and a heartfelt gratitude for their compassion towards us and the dedication to their work.

We were to meet the detective again when he travelled up to see Gary. He gave us an update on the proceedings and he said he would let us know when the time came for the trial. He was obviously pleased to see Gary and was able to ask him some unanswered questions. He also brought with him some personal belongings of Gary's from the flat. The next time we met him was at the trial.

It was such a relief to have Gary home. Even though he was in hospital I only had to travel ten minutes down the road and now he was conscious I was able to talk to him. I knew that he would live, so there was a future and Gary would be part of it. I hoped that it would be the beginning of things getting back to normal.

On my first visit we spent the best part of it crying. I don't know who cried the most, but it was certainly a tearful reunion. Gary found it very difficult to come to terms with his disability, and although I was heartbroken, I did nothing but encourage him to look forward. To my mind the worst was over and I told him that from then on things would start to get better. It was a very depressing time for Gary. He had suffered so much and all he could see in front of him was more suffering. But I couldn't allow him to dwell on the bad side of things and was determined myself to adopt a positive attitude.

* * *

Shelagh and I had returned to work, so things were getting back to normal. It took Shelagh longer because it wasn't until she returned home that she started to grieve for her partner. She had been so preoccupied with her brother that she hadn't had time to come to terms with her own loss, so it was a few weeks later that she was able to return to her work in Manchester. However, the owner of the petrol stations sold up and moved abroad soon after our return so we were both out of a job.

Gary continued to make slow progress and he remained in hospital for about three weeks; during which time we did our best to ensure that at least one member of the family was with him during visiting hours. He was up and sitting in a wheelchair so we often found him in the television room and we were able to take him to the hospital's café and restaurant.

He was finally moved to the rehabilitation unit, which is situated in the grounds of Burnley General Hospital. The prime concern was to straighten out his feet so that he could walk. It wasn't possible to do anything with his right arm and hand as there was nothing there to work on, but the physiotherapist who worked with Gary said he had every reason to believe that he could get him walking again.

It was a long and painful journey and there were times when Gary refused to have physio. His right foot was so badly twisted it was hard to believe that he would be able to walk on it. I recall on a number of occasions, the physiotherapist sought me out to ask me to have a word with Gary because he was not cooperating. It was what I would call an on/off relationship, but neither of them gave up and the end result was a success.

The specialist at the hospital made a calliper for Gary's right leg and he had a shoe that was specially adapted to fit Gary's foot. With these and the help of a walking aid in his left hand, he was able to take a few steps. It was a lengthy process, during which the calliper had to be adjusted or the shoe altered until everything fitted just right. Once this was achieved he was able to walk a bit further each day, albeit a bit lopsided.

Gary was never renowned for his patience and it wasn't long before he asked to come home. I think they would have liked to keep him longer, but he was adamant that he could manage, so he was discharged and went to stay at Shelagh's house. After a time he rented a two-bedroom terraced house and I stayed with him for a few days to help him settle in. He wasn't there for long when he was offered a bungalow that had been specially adapted for disabled people.

* * *

Prior to Gary sustaining his horrific injuries, Eddie and I had enjoyed a comfortable life. I had a job that paid well and twice a year we travelled abroad to Portugal and Spain. On each occasion we took one or two of the grandchildren, which made the holidays more expensive. I wouldn't say we were living the 'good life', but we were certainly making the most of life. I had the usual credit cards and a car loan that I could well afford to pay each month.

All this came to a sudden stop when Gary was attacked. Spending weeks on end travelling back and forth to the hospital had become a serious strain on my credit facilities. Neither Shelagh nor I had wages coming in and Shelagh didn't have any credit cards. By the time I returned home I had received demand letters from all my creditors.

Fortunately Eddie's name wasn't on any of my financial transactions. Eventually we had to sell the house and I had to declare myself bankrupt. I was very upset; not just for me, but for Eddie in particular. Although he had enjoyed the pleasures of life alongside me, he had in no way been responsible for the amount of debts incurred due to what happened to Gary and it was due to these that we had to face the loss of our home. I don't recall him blaming me in any way at all, but it was a big setback. I couldn't afford a lawyer so made an appointment to see Citizens Advice. The woman I saw was very good and agreed to represent me in court. I had to find two hundred pounds to file for the bankruptcy papers. Shelagh went to the court with me, and I don't know which of us was the most nervous. It had been a time of worry and stress leading up to the day. I felt like a criminal, but when I left the building I was very relieved. All my debts had been wiped off and I vowed there and then I would never own another credit card or take on a loan ever again. To this day I never have.

* * *

Eventually we received a letter from the Crown Prosecution Service informing us about the trial. It was detailed in their weird and wonderful jargon which, when translated, told us who the QC was, what the charges were, the date and place of the trial and where we could find accommodation if we wished to attend.

It was about twelve months since we were down in Devon, and on this occasion I travelled with my daughter and my son and it was a much happier journey than the previous one. We stayed in a bed and breakfast in Plymouth, so we wouldn't have far to travel to Plymouth Crown Court each day.

When we went into the courtroom it was like entering a whole new world. We immediately started whispering as if on sacred ground. I tried to weigh up who was who. I knew the people behind me were the general public; I surmised that those in front of me were the relations of the accused as they were seated near the box where Gary's attackers would be placed when they entered the court. In the centre of the room were two desks; one for the prosecution and one for the defence. To the side was a smaller table which would be occupied by the stenographer. Men in black robes came in and out; placing papers on tables and picking papers up, but the show didn't get underway until the 'wigs' came in and someone said, 'Be upstanding in court,' at which we all got to our feet while we watched the man who could change people's lives take a seat. His seat was much higher up than anyone else's; whether it was so that he could look down on us or we could look up to him, I am not sure. The deadly silence was broken when we were informed that the court was in session.

The two accused were led into the courtroom by a prison officer. When they were seated I took a good look at them and what I felt was a sense of disappointment. They looked like any other young men on the street. They were clean shaven and well dressed. One was about twenty-three and the other about eighteen; they certainly didn't look like I expected drug addicts and attempted murderers to look. It became obvious that people cannot be judged by appearances alone. Gary didn't speak or move when he saw them, and he never discussed with me his feelings because he was too emotionally involved.

During the lunch break we had sandwiches and coffee and we sort of mingled. I was aware of the presence of the parents of the accused, especially the mother of one of them because when the men were led into court she started crying. It was apparent that one couple was very upset and the other couple were doing their best to comfort them. I was conscious of their presence and the strained atmosphere; it was clearly a case of 'us and them'. I had no desire to speak to any of them, but it became apparent that the mother who was crying had previously spoken to Gary and wanted to convey to us how sorry she was. Personally I wasn't in a position to accommodate her, and I don't know if Shelagh couldn't or wouldn't speak to them.

It was a long, tiring day. The proceedings in the courtroom were long and drawn-out, and I didn't understand half of it. I was glad when it was adjourned until the next day; besides which, the seat was rock hard and I had a numb backside. On the way home we spoke about the strangeness of it all; like being on another planet, only I didn't know if we were aliens or they were. All I knew was that my family and I had entered a whole new world and I didn't like it one bit.

As the trial proceeded I found it very hard going. I didn't like the environment or the people who moved in these circles. I rebelled against the officialdom; in particular what I considered to be the high-minded, pompous attitude of those representing the law and believing themselves to be a breed apart. When they had to convey knowledge gained during the court proceedings that had to be translated into the working-class dialogue, they had great difficulty in finding a level in which they could converse with the likes of me.

After a very arduous week, endless cups of coffee and unappetising sandwiches, the trial reached its final day in which the judge was to give his summing up, his deliberation and ultimately his final judgement and sentencing. I can't say that we learnt much from the trial, mainly because everything was so alien – what was relevant to them was irrelevant to us. As we all became 'upstanding' for the last time, the judge proceeded to sum up in detail all that had taken place in the courtroom from day one up until present time; at the end of which, he found the accused guilty and sentenced them both to ten years in prison.

Knowing they wouldn't serve the full ten years, I thought that was pretty lenient considering that my son had a lifetime sentence of being disabled, but I was content to know that they were going to pay for what they had done and was more than happy to exit the courtroom knowing that I would not have to return. It was all over and done with – what a relief – we could all get back to normal again.

We asked Gary's QC about compensation. He said that the Criminal Injuries Board had changed the rules about compensation and they had a new ruling that stated any person with a criminal record would no longer be entitled to criminal compensation. I explained that Gary had already been punished for his past crimes and had no violence on his records at all. He said we could always try to challenge the new ruling, but we probably wouldn't win.

I had no intention of going down that road: by that stage I'd had enough of the judicial system. I still think the ruling is wrong. As far as I was concerned, they were saying because he had got into trouble at some point in his life, he wasn't worthy of any compensation, even though his injures had totally changed every aspect of his life.

Keith had recorded the television news about Gary, thinking that he would be able to see the recordings when he felt up to it. He never did see them: when I played the tape for him he started crying and told me to switch it off.

We left Devon with an untold gratitude to Keith and his wife, without whom we would have been at a loss. On returning home we settled down to a normal way of life. I found work in a local petrol station; Shelagh also started work at the same place.

My son settled into his new bungalow and when he had saved up enough money, I decided to take him abroad. He had never been abroad before and I wanted him to have a quality of life worth living. We went to Ibiza with my grandson, Damien. Gary basked in the sun all day and partied all night long. I had never seen him so happy. He even took up with a lady friend who was boarding at the same hotel, so I didn't see much of him in the evenings, but he always came to see if I was alright, and made a point of looking after me.

I was taken ill one morning with terrible stomach cramps. Gary went down to reception to ask for a doctor. When the doctor came, she examined me, gave me a prescription and then told me that I owed her fifty pounds. We argued over this as I thought the insurance should cover it; besides which, she had only spent a few minutes of her time with me. She didn't persist, so we didn't have to pay in the end. Gary went out to find a chemist to get the prescription. He set off with Damien and didn't come back for two hours. He had walked nearly two miles in search of a chemist. Damien said he kept telling Gary they had to turn back, but he wouldn't give up until he found one. He was sweating and had an abrasion on his leg where his calliper had rubbed it sore, but he had a bottle of medicine in his hand.

When we returned home he had one aim in life, and that was to save as much as he could of his disability allowance so he could travel abroad. He did this over a period of two years and went to Tunisia twice a year before tragedy struck yet again.

Chapter Nine

IHADN'T AT ANY TIME DURING my life thought to write my life story, but when Shelagh bought me a typewriter and said I should write it, I kept looking at the typewriter for a few weeks before I finally decided to do it. I determined from the onset to neither add nor take away, but to tell it as it evolved. I didn't realise at that time the effect it would have on me and the effort I would have to put into the telling of it. Some days have passed since I last sat at my typewriter because I have been struggling to come to terms with the next episode of my life and have wondered if I am able to relate the events that follow. I even reached a point when I thought to give it all up and forget about it. My final decision was that I should make a start and see how it goes. If I can't handle it, I will cross that bridge when I come to it.

* * *

I was on holiday with Eddie. We were staying with Keith and had just returned from a lovely day out on Dartmoor when the phone rang.

Keith came back into the living room. 'It's Shelagh on the phone.'

Unknown to me at that stage, she had told him what had happened and asked him to watch out for my reaction as the last time something bad had happened I had refused to acknowledge it.

I knew she had planned to take Gary out for the day to a special event for the disabled at Rimmington. He had been the year before and had had a great time on an electric wheelchair, so was looking forward to going again. She told me that Gary had gone on an electric wheelchair, that the chair had overturned and Gary had been thrown out. He had landed on the concrete road, unable to protect himself because he had landed on the side where he had no use. His head had taken the full impact.

The nearest hospital didn't have the facilities to deal with Gary's injuries, so he had been transferred to Hope Hospital in Manchester and she had followed by car. The surgeon had told her that Gary's head injuries had caused internal bleeding and they wouldn't know the extent of the damage until they had operated. I told Shelagh I would be home the next day.

Somehow, among all the tears, Eddie and I made the decision to travel home overnight. We arrived in the early morning and went to the hospital with Shelagh.

As we entered the ward I stopped and broke down crying. Once again I found myself leaning against a hospital wall for support.

'I can't do this,' I said to Shelagh.

'You have to, Mum.'

On reflection, I didn't consider how my daughter was coping. I was so consumed with what was happening to Gary, my failure to deal with the trauma it caused me, that I was incapable of thinking of how it affected her. She not only had to deal with her own emotions concerning her brother, but she also had to deal with a mother who was slowly falling apart. She was, and is, undoubtedly one of a kind.

When I finally managed to pull myself together, I walked into the ward and approached the bed where my son lay. I had done the exact same thing two years ago. He lay motionless, his head heavily covered in bandages.

This was history repeating itself, I thought. It couldn't be happening again, it's not fair. Once more I was crying, only this time it was heart wrenching; more so because I knew that the damage to Gary's brain was far greater than the previous damage.

The surgeon who operated on Gary said that because the skin had not broken at the time of the fall, it had bled inwards, causing severe damage to the brain. He had done all he could to repair that damage, but they wouldn't know until, or even if, Gary recovered to what extent the damage would cause overall. Complete paralysis – partial paralysis – memory loss – inability to speak. All I could think was that he had bled for eight hours: from the time the wheelchair toppled over to the time they operated. We were in serious trouble.

To this day, I don't know why it took so long from the time of his injury to the time of operating. Shelagh said that when the ambulance arrived it took three men to constrain him. This surely should have told them of possible head injury, yet they took him to a hospital that was unable to deal with him, and all the time he was bleeding on the brain, causing more and more damage. It appeared to me there was no urgency throughout the whole episode. I've watched programmes on television and seen helicopters airlifting people who have been involved in accidents and heard the paramedics saying how vital it is to get them to surgery as soon as possible if head injuries are involved. I've asked myself the same question again and again: 'Why did it take eight hours?' knowing that had it taken two, three, or even four hours, the damage may not have been as severe.

Each day, along with my family, I travelled back and forth to the hospital – a journey of about forty minutes each way. It wasn't as far as the journey down in Devon, but it was nonetheless just as tiring and depressing.

I sat by his bedside every day, holding his hand and talking to him. I didn't know if he could hear me or not, but I continued to talk to him just in case. He showed no kind of movement or sign of life. He was fed by a drip and had a tracheotomy to help with his breathing, and for easy access should they need it.

During those days and weeks that I sat by his bed, I constantly reflected on his life. He'd had to contend with so much during his life. I know he had suffered while he was in prison. I thought back to the time when we had visited him and found another inmate had cut his wrists. I recalled the time when I was watching Gary in a queue and one of the inmates jumped the queue in front of him. He was a big strapping lad and Gary stood up to him. A person has to know when to back off and let things go, but Gary hadn't learnt that lesson. I told him when he came and sat back down, and he said, 'But he shouldn't do that, Mum.' I knew then that he was going to have problems.

When he got married I thought he'd had the chance to settle down, but he didn't. He shot off and, from what I could gather, he moved from pillar to post until he finished up in prison near Newton Abbott in Devon. It was while he was serving a two-year sentence there that he applied to Plymouth University. He passed the necessary exams, the university found him some accommodation, and he was studying Statistics and Geography when he was attacked by the two men in his flat.

Now he lay on this bed with brain damage. The surgeon said he had never come across anyone before with two brain injuries. I dreaded the outcome. What would he be like when he came to? I know he had been to prison, but he had never hurt anyone in his life. Why was this happening? It was like something out of a horror movie. We were just ordinary people; not built to deal with such trauma. I'd already been through this – I struggled to get through the first ordeal and I was being asked to go through it all again: all the heartbreak, all the tears and that awful feeling of knowing I could do nothing but watch a loved one suffer. I thought I knew all about suffering. How wrong can a person be?

I have often thought, looking back, where does the breaking point come? How much are we able to bear? Because when it comes down to it, we reach that point in our lives when we can no longer carry on: the pain, the grief, the suffering is all too much. It was when I arrived at that point where I could no longer endure it, that I began to look for a way out. I thought about getting some tablets and taking myself and Gary out of it. But then I realised that I couldn't do it. And then came the acceptance, and along with it the ability to carry on. I knew it was going to be a long journey and my constant companion would be the heartache of watching a loved one suffer, but I also knew I could and would carry on. No matter what the cost I would carry on because what I had found out ultimately was that it was not more than I could bear.

When Gary finally recovered consciousness he was completely paralysed. He couldn't move and he couldn't talk, and we didn't know if he could see or hear; all we knew was he could cry.

When I look back on this time of my life, I don't know how I survived, I don't know how my son survived; and my lovely daughter – her partner dead, her brother disabled, and a mother who was literally in pieces. When Shelagh had said to me, 'You have no choice', well, that's it in a nutshell; we had no choice and just had to carry on as best we could.

The consultant surgeon said he didn't think there would be any improvement in Gary's condition and there was nothing further they could do to help him. They tried sitting him up in a chair by the side of his bed, but I don't believe he knew where he was or what had happened to him. He was out of intensive care and we visited every day to spend time with him and talk to him, but there was no sign of improvement.

After a number of weeks we arranged for Gary to be transferred to Burnley General Hospital. He was placed in a single room which led off from a main ward. Every day I went in to see him. He was propped up in bed and the pores all over his body were not exactly sweating, but more like pouring. I didn't know what was going on; we weren't even sure if he could see, but we suspected he could because whenever the nurse came in to take a sample of blood – which was every day – Gary's body tensed up as she entered the room. When I asked why it was necessary to take blood so often, they said they were trying to find out what was happening in order to treat it as the brain was sending wrong messages to his body.

Looking back on this later with Eddie, we agreed we should have put a stop to it because they never did treat him, and the final decision they made was to send for my husband and I to attend a meeting. The meeting was with the consultant and a senior nurse. They told us they thought it best to stop feeding Gary and to let him die.

'There is no way you can do that while Gary is fighting to live,' I said and walked out. I stood outside, crying.

The nurse came out. 'We thought you had realised that Gary would never recover.'

'No, I didn't realise it, and I don't accept it either.'

ONE OF A KIND

When I had recovered slightly, I went back into the room.

'As far as I'm concerned,' I said, 'your suggestion is in no way acceptable and if you can't treat him, then I'll find someone who can.'

I went home and rang Shelagh at work. I told her what had happened, sobbing my heart out. They hadn't given Gary a chance, I said. He could start recovering and miracles still happened.

I set about looking for answers. I contacted the consultant at Rakehead Rehabilitation Unit where Gary had spent time recovering from his previous injuries. He went to see Gary, but he said they couldn't do anything for him. Eventually a rehab centre in Bury, just outside Manchester, agreed to take him. They had a good reputation for treating victims suffering from brain damage and other head injuries. I was pleased he was leaving Burnley General where I thought they had been too previous in giving up on him. The lesson I learnt from this was to never assume those with degrees and letters to their name know what is best for me or my loved ones, because it is not always the case.

We visited Gary regularly at the rehab centre. At first it was very upsetting because he didn't seem to be making any progress. I can't say how much I suffered during this period. It was heartbreaking to see Gary lying there, unable to speak or move, those tear-filled eyes looking at me, pleading for me to help him. The fact that I was so helpless only added to what I felt to be a failure on my part. I still didn't know if he could hear me, but every time I saw him I told him what I had determined in my heart: 'Don't worry, Gary, I am going to bring you home.' I asked him later if he had heard me and he indicated that he had.

Gary slowly began to improve. His carers sat him up in bed and before long they had him in a wheelchair, so when we came to visit we were able to take him out for a walk. He didn't respond to any of the games or activities, but we had discovered that he could hear, which was a big step forward because it meant we could correspond. He nodded his head for yes and shook his head for no. Then we found out something which was truly amazing: he still had a great sense of humour. After all he had been through and the condition he found himself in, he could laugh. For the first time I felt that there was hope.

After some time we began talking to Gary about coming home. We had a good idea of what this would involve, but all family members had agreed that we wanted him home, no matter what it entailed. Needless to say, Gary wanted to come home; in fact it's a wonder his head didn't fall off it was going up and down at such a rate. We talked it over with the powers that be and an appointment was made for a meeting to take place to discuss the matter.

When the day arrived, Eddie, Shelagh and I were very optimistic and very determined to put a strong case for bringing Gary home. When we were called in there was a very large table with about eight people seated round it. They all nodded and smiled at us as we sat down. The head of the rehab centre opened the meeting by thanking us for coming. She said they had discussed the possibility of Gary returning home and then she put forward all the reasons why Gary would not be allowed to go home. He was paralysed, he was being fed by peg tube, he had a tracheostomy in his throat, and he needed 24-hour care.

We challenged all these issues: we were well aware of his condition and were willing and able to look after him. But we slowly began to realise that they had already made the decision not to allow him home, and that this had been arrived at before we even entered the room. We might as well not have been there: it was a complete waste of time and a deception in the sense that they had led us to believe that it may be possible. We came away angry and disillusioned.

The whole scene reminded me of the court house at Plymouth: all sitting there, each representing their own departments, each believing themselves to be of importance. It wasn't about what was actually best for Gary; it was about what *they* thought was best for him. I had never felt so inadequate in my life. I knew they were not going to budge, but the knowledge that they had made the decision without even consulting us made us angry.

The head of the rehab centre said, 'Gary is not able to swallow.'

I looked at Gary, who was sitting at the end of the table. His Adam's apple was going up and down, trying to tell them he could swallow. I pointed this out to her, but she said that Gary didn't understand the implications involved.

'Yes he does, and so do the family, and we want him home,' I retorted.

'It isn't possible. It isn't just my decision, but all those present. You should respect our decision.'

I couldn't believe that his social worker, who had led us to believe we could rely on his support, sided with those present. When we challenged him afterwards he said he hadn't realised the serious implications involved with Gary and he couldn't condone his release. I believe what he meant was he didn't want to lose his job if he backed us up and we came unstuck!

I decided not to let the powers that be convince me that Gary would be better looked after in a home. I felt I could do a better job than they could. There is nothing that can beat a one-to-one relationship whose foundation is love.

Talk about fate intervening: Gary was taken ill and admitted to Bury General Hospital with a chest infection. This soon turned into pneumonia and he was placed in intensive care. The doctor told us they had administered as many antibiotics as they possibly could and didn't know if Gary would pull through. All we could do was pray.

Although it seemed at the time to be another crisis to overcome, in actual fact it turned out to be a blessing in disguise. When Gary recovered – albeit slowly – we began to notice a marked improvement. He was much more alert and he indicated that he wanted his tracheostomy tube taking out. The doctor said because Gary had such a strong cough he was willing to remove it. He asked Gary if he were to choke if he wanted resuscitating. Once again Gary's head moved up and down very rapidly.

The tube was removed, as a result of which the rehab centre refused to take him back. They were not willing to take responsibility as they considered he deliberately put himself at risk. Because the improvement was so apparent, Shelagh and I knew what the next move was to be.

Doreen Salmon

We contacted the consultant in charge of Rakehead Rehabilitation Unit and pleaded Gary's cause. He agreed to go and see him. I was very optimistic and very grateful that he was willing to go. I knew he was a very busy man and from past experience knew him to be a very dedicated man towards his patients.

When he walked into the room, Gary recognised him right away. He gave Gary a thorough examination, at the end of which he said he couldn't believe he was the same person he saw in Burnley General. He was truly surprised at the change in him and said that he would give serious consideration as to whether Gary would benefit by being admitted to Rakehead and, depending on the availability of a bed, he would notify the doctor that Gary was presently under his decision. We didn't know what that decision would be, but to say that we were hopeful would be a big understatement.

* * *

The other good thing that happened to Gary was a wonderful physiotherapist who collected him from his room each day and took him to a gymnasium to exercise his limbs with great enthusiasm. She moved his legs as he found he could raise them slightly. He could also move his body from the waist up, backwards and forwards, and he found he had most movement in his left arm and hand. On the downside, he couldn't sit up without falling over and there was no movement in his lower back.

Gary had been in Bury Hospital for about six weeks when word came through that Rakehead would take him. He was on the first rung of the ladder towards going home. I found Bury Hospital a very caring environment during the time Gary spent there. It is a period that I can reflect on with a smile because it was a good time in which Gary found he could still laugh.

I started looking forward to going to see him. I could start believing that Gary was going to have a life that would be worth living after all. Of course, he had a long way to go but it was a definite turning point and I truly believe it was because of the care he received from both nurses and doctors at Bury, not to mention the peace of mind I found with him being there.

* * *

Gary was to remain in Rakehead for over a year. During that time he had a room of his own and the staff concentrated on his physical disabilities and his health in general. Although he had arrived at Rakehead without a tracheostomy tube, when the hole began to heal I realised that he might choke and they would have no access to help him to breathe. I panicked. I discussed with the consultant the possibility of putting the tube back in and he agreed that it would be safer for Gary to have it replaced. I remember the nurse who went with him to have it replaced stayed with him that night and lay on the bed to comfort him because he was so upset. I hadn't realised how painful it would be for him and I felt responsible because it was at my instigation that it be replaced.

The nurses got Gary up every morning, got him washed and dressed, and took him to the main area where all the residents assembled. There were around six or seven other residents, but Gary didn't mix with them. One reason was that he couldn't talk, but he didn't seem to want to mix; he preferred to be in his room where he could watch what he liked on the television. So when we visited him in the afternoons we always knew where to find him.

We were able to communicate with Gary much better. We learnt how to present things to him in a certain way so that he only had to nod or shake his head. The speech therapist discussed with Gary and his family the different methods of communication that were available and which ones she thought would be most beneficial to Gary. We settled on a Dynavox communicator, in which sentences could be inputted. This proved to be an invaluable lifeline for Gary; he took to it like a duck to water. Page after page of words and phrases were inputted, and he was able to find the words and bring them up with the use of his left hand. He was coming out of his cocoon and back into a life that we all hoped would be worth the living.

After Gary had been there for some time, we brought up the question of taking him home: he was always asking for this. The bungalow he was living in at the time of his accident was owned by the local housing association and we had managed to keep it going for him through trial and error. The bungalow was specially adapted for a disabled person so there wasn't a problem so far as accommodation went. The problem was finding cover for him as he needed 24-hour care. They said they didn't think I would be able to look after him because of my age, which at that time was sixty-five. Shelagh said she would give up work and help to look after Gary, but I knew I could do it and I didn't want Shelagh tied to Gary for what could be many years. I wanted her to have a normal life for as long as possible because when I could no longer manage Gary, she would then have to take over.

While Gary was in Rakehead we engaged a solicitor to look into compensation for Gary with regard to what happened at Rimmington. It was a special event which was run by the water company and we believed that they should be held responsible for the events that took place. As it turned out they denied all responsibility, and the man in charge of the wheelchairs said that although he had arranged for the wheelchairs to be there he was not insured, so there was no point in pursuing a man who didn't have the means to compensate Gary. Nevertheless, we did our upmost to get the water company to acknowledge that it was their event and as such they were responsible. As with all such conglomerates, they were quick enough to take our money, but when it came to paying out they didn't want to know. To add insult to injury, they sent letters of demand for water that had been lost due to burst pipes while Gary was in hospital as a result of attending an event which they had held. Had it not been so tragic, I might be amused by the irony of it.

* * *

When the time came for Rakehead to make a decision as to Gary's future, a meeting was held that consisted of all relevant members of staff, family and social services. On this occasion no conclusion had been reached prior to our arrival.

It was obvious from the onset that all present – with the exception of family – thought the best place for Gary was in a home: it was up to us to persuade them otherwise. One argument was based on the experience that I had of working in homes for the elderly and the abuse I had witnessed at first hand. My daughter had also worked with the elderly and had, along with myself, reported incidents of abuse which were duly noted, never dealt with in a proper manner and frowned upon by fellow workers. This only strengthened our resolve to prevent Gary being placed in a care home. No matter how good a reputation a home may have, there might be at least one bad apple, and that is one too many.

I was told that before any decisions could be reached I would have to prove to them that I was capable of looking after Gary. I was to report to Rakehead five days a week for two weeks, nine to five. I was to wash him, shave him, toilet him, dress him, get him up and put him back to bed each day – with the help of a nurse for lifting purposes only. I agreed right away, and not only did I do as they had requested, but I enjoyed looking after my son. What mother wouldn't?

* * *

It was towards the end of the first week of attending to Gary that Eddie had a heart attack.

He was rushed into Burnley General Hospital where he was admitted to the intensive care unit. He had no previous record of heart trouble so it came as a big shock to us all. He was kept on the unit for two days while his heart was monitored, after which he was moved onto a ward. I was not only upset, but I was worried because I didn't know where it was leading, and I didn't know anything about the procedure or what it entailed. After about a week he was allowed home and was referred to a heart specialist in Manchester where he was to undergo tests.

As a result of Eddie being admitted to hospital, it meant that I was looking after my son during the day, and visiting my husband at night. This, as it turned out, went in my favour because at the end of the two weeks they had allocated to me as a trial run, I passed with flying colours. They were no longer in doubt as to whether or not I could look after Gary: they were now absolutely certain that I could. A further meeting was arranged to discuss the next move towards taking Gary home.

When Eddie attended Manchester Royal Hospital for tests I went with him. The results showed that he had five blocked arteries and needed five bypasses. Shortly afterwards he was given a date for the operation.

I knew it was going to be a stressful time. Not only would I have the responsibility of visiting my husband every day and the worry of the operation, but also I didn't want to let Gary down. He was used to seeing me every day, so I arranged for Shelagh, who was in full-time employment, to visit Gary every evening. When I explained the situation to Gary he nodded, indicating that it was alright and he had a good cry in sympathy with his stepfather.

Because I knew I was facing a difficult time worrying over Eddie, wondering if he was going to be alright – bearing in mind that he was now seventy years old and knowing that it was going to be very painful for him – I was beginning to realise that I wasn't going to be able to deal with this. There was also all the travelling to Manchester and back each day on my own, so I did the only thing I could think of. I rang Keith and asked him if he could come up for a few days. I knew that my sister-in-law was suffering from leukaemia, but at that time she was managing quite well so it seemed the right thing to do. He came up right away and was a blessing. He took over, made light of everything and made me laugh. We got lost in Manchester nearly every time; although he always insisted he knew where he was going. The funny part about it was that he had lived in Manchester for a number of years.

He stayed with me until Eddie came home from hospital. When we had done visiting at the hospital we returned home and spent each evening playing cards. When we were young we went with our parents every weekend to their friends and they always played cards for money – not vast amounts, just pennies really. So we had an early schooling in gambling and still play whenever we meet up. I am very proud he is my brother.

Keith is always boasting about how he is never ill and stays out in the rain trying to catch a cold. He phoned me up recently to tell me he had been to the hospital and had a camera down his throat. He said if he had known how bad it was going to be, he wouldn't have gone. He said he had been having stomach trouble, however on this occasion he said he wouldn't have minded but he only went to the doctors because he had earache!

Eddie's operation went very well, though he was in considerable pain. This was understandable, having had five bypasses. The thing I found strange was when he was sitting in his bedside chair, he kept bending down as though he was picking things up. When I asked him what he was doing, he said exactly that: he was picking things up off the floor, even though there was nothing there. I found out later that they had asked him if he would volunteer to try a new anaesthetic. Had I known about this I would have advised him to say no: 'never volunteer' is an old army saying. I put his strange behaviour down to the new anaesthetic.

After being in hospital for about a week, he was allowed home, but he wasn't well and it took him a long time to recover. During those months we'd had to have our dog Clyde put down. He had always gone everywhere with my husband so it was a very upsetting time for him and as he was in a weak condition he wasn't able to overcome the loss very easily.

* * *

Although it was accepted that I was capable of looking after Gary, we had to have several meetings in order to put together a care package. The package consisted of Primary Care Trust (PCT) staff, social services and family. This provided 24-hour care and, although it was pretty straightforward for family, the PCT staff had to be trained for Gary's special needs. This took some months.

Doreen Salmon

We had to have the bathroom altered for Gary. This involved taking the bath out and installing a shower he could use with a shower trolley. He also needed a special bed and mattress, a hoist and a wheelchair.

The week he was due home we ordered all his medication and feeds, and finally we ordered the ambulance to bring him home. What a momentous occasion it was. When Gary had turned the key in his front door to go out for a day out, it was to be four years before he returned. We had achieved what we thought at times would be impossible through sheer determination and faith in a living God.

Chapter Ten

Gary has been home for five years and I have only recently handed over the responsibility of looking after him to Shelagh. The past five years have been a pleasure for me to look after Gary. Although he often gets stressed, he has a wonderful sense of humour. It never fails to amaze me after all he has been through that he is taking control of his life, making his own decisions, and has created a way of life which gives him the best quality possible.

It hasn't been easy for me over the past years. When Gary first came home we had lots of staff problems, with people not turning up or going off sick. I seemed to receive phone calls on a regular basis saying someone hadn't turned up, and although I had been with him all day I'd have to go back and fill in until Shelagh could get there.

The biggest upset was when Gary went into respite for two weeks. We couldn't find a disabled unit that was able to take him, so he went into a nursing home. While he was there, one of the staff pulled his feeding tube out and Gary had to go into hospital to have it replaced. When they put the new tube in they set up a feeding drip. Gary knew this would cause him to be sick, as we had discovered while he was in Rakehead. No one had thought to take Gary's communicator with him, so he was unable to tell them. So he told them the only way he knew how, and that was by pulling the peg tube out. As a result of this he was not fed.

When I arrived back from holiday I went to see Gary and found he had retreated back into his shell. He had been lying there for five days without a feed or water, no air bed, no television. I won't relate what I said to the so-called nurses. Suffice to say, he got an air bed straightaway and his peg tube was put back in the following day.

I brought him home the day after that. His mouth was so full of ulcers I couldn't get a syringe in to give him water. Needless to say, he has a caption on his communicator which states 'Under no circumstances am I to be admitted to hospital'. We have since found him a place for respite in a special disabled unit where he is well cared for.

The last twelve years of my life have been dedicated to looking after my son and now, having passed a lifespan of three score years and ten, I find myself more or less a lady of leisure.

I have much to be thankful for. I have a wonderful daughter who did everything possible to ease the burden for me and has now taken up the mantle that I have lain down. I have a husband who has loved and comforted me through the years, and I have a son who I was told wouldn't live, but who is now living life to the full. I also have a loving brother and four grandsons who are all I could wish for and more.

Over the last three years we have done our utmost to find Gary's children, Benjamin and Emma, who he buys birthday cards and Christmas cards for every year. We have contacted different chat shows and the local newspaper in Warrington where Gary's ex-wife, Susan, came from, and although the newspaper ran a story on Gary with all the details available, we received no response. The children will be around nineteen years old now and I've told Gary that I hope they will come looking for him. Susan will not be aware of Gary's further injuries and the twins probably aren't aware of their father's disabilities.

Once we have found them, or they have found him, our family will be complete. It will be a very happy reunion when they finally meet up.

At this present time we are looking into the possibility of Gary staying at home for his six weeks' respite each year, instead of going to the special disabled unit. Problems have arisen with regard to the quality of care. It's not easy when a person is used to a one-to-one caring atmosphere at home, and then has to adapt to a new routine in a home. Gary is very set in his routine and finds it hard to handle change. Because he is unable to speak, it is very difficult to understand why he asks to stay at home, but we do know Gary is under 24-hour care because he is at risk and if Gary feels he doesn't receive adequate care, then he had every right to ask for the same care he gets at home.

We have just returned from taking Gary on his first holiday in years. We did look into taking him abroad but the cost was astronomical so we ended up taking him to Blackpool for two weeks in a specially adapted caravan. Gary really enjoyed the break but as usual the good old British weather spoilt it! We are still hoping to get Gary abroad at some time in the future, finances allowing, as this is his dream.

We have also got Gary a wheelchair-accessible vehicle so he has a lot more freedom. He has started going to church about once a fortnight and I do believe it won't be long before his outlook on life will be greatly improved and this will be a blessing to us all.

Now that my life story is coming to an end it only leaves me to recount the part I have thus far omitted. I can take no credit for lasting out the heartbreaking years I endured with my son. Jesus was my constant companion; ever present, encouraging me to carry on and strengthening me each day with the knowledge that love conquers all. To my mind and that of my family, this has been proven to be true, for it was love that brought Gary home.

If I were at liberty to tell more I would do so. Perhaps if God spares me, there will be another story to tell. In the meantime let me close with the words my friend said to me all those years ago:

Read the Gospel according to Saint John and find the friend of a lifetime.